LILLIAN TOO
& JENNIFER TOO
fortune & feng shui
2008
DOG

Published by KONSEP LAGENDA SDN BHD (223 855)
Kuala Lumpur 59100 Malaysia.
Websites: www.lillian-too.com • www.wofs.com
Email: webmaster@wofs.com

Lillian Too & Jennifer Too
Fortune & Feng Shui 2008 DOG
© Konsep Lagenda Sdn Bhd

Editorial Director: Jennifer Too
Creative Director: Cheryl Chow
Designers & Illustrators: Andrew Yep, Adeline Chen,
Jackye Seng, Jeannie Yue & Calvin Liew

ISBN   9 7 8 - 9 8 3 - 3 2 6 3 - 8 5 - 1
Published in Malaysia
October 2007

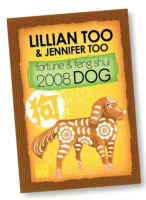

LILLIAN TOO
& JENNIFER TOO
fortune & feng shui
2008 DOG

LILLIAN TOO
& JENNIFER TOO
fortune & feng shui
2008 BOAR

LILLIAN TOO
& JENNIFER TOO
fortune & feng shui
2008 RAT

LILLIAN TOO
& JENNIFER TOO
fortune & feng shui
2008 OX

LILLIAN TOO
& JENNIFER TOO
fortune & feng shui
2008 TIGER

LILLIAN TOO
& JENNIFER TOO
fortune & feng shui
2008 RABBIT

LILLIAN TOO
& JENNIFER TOO
fortune & feng shui
2008 DRAGON

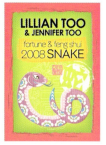

LILLIAN TOO
& JENNIFER TOO
fortune & feng shui
2008 SNAKE

LILLIAN TOO
& JENNIFER TOO
fortune & feng shui
2008 HORSE

LILLIAN TOO
& JENNIFER TOO
fortune & feng shui
2008 SHEEP

LILLIAN TOO
& JENNIFER TOO
fortune & feng shui
2008 MONKEY

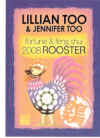

LILLIAN TOO
& JENNIFER TOO
fortune & feng shui
2008 ROOSTER

Contents

Introduction

THE 24 MOUNTAIN FORTUNE STARS

The fortune stars exert strong influences on the annual chart, affecting not only the luck of the animal signs but also impacting on the feng shui of houses. In all, there are 108 different types of fortune stars that fly into the 24 mountains. These differ in type and possess different strengths according to the year they fly in. Some bring good luck, some convey misfortune, while others carry special protection or luck to the animal sign residing there. It also affects the luck of houses that face or sit in that direction.

Each of the twelve books in this series contains explanations on the fortune star that affects them and their houses. These stars weaken or strengthen the *chi* energies of the animal sign and when the annual energies are afflicted, having them weakened is a good thing. When negative

t o commemorate the new zodiac cycle, which starts in the current year of the Earth Rat, we are expanding this year's forecast readings to incorporate the stars that fly into the 24 mountains of the feng shui compass. This offers extra analysis for each of the animal signs and brings new dimensions to your feng shui updates.

afflicted energies lose strength they are not as lethal as when they are strong.

When the annual energies are auspicious however, it is better when they are strengthened. When they get weakened, they need strengthening elements in place to add extra vigour, otherwise the good fortune essence cannot manifest.

TWELVE SOLAR MONTHS

The monthly readings also incorporate the influence of the luck pillars of each month to add greater substance to the analysis of good and bad months. You will find this year's fortunes and feng shui of the twelve animal signs to be more detailed and helpful in alerting you to negative afflictions.

This adds to the benefits of staying updated on the changing *chi* of the year

and helps you take correct precautions to guard against misfortune, illness and aggravations. Being forewarned is forearmed and usually the remedies are so easy to put in place and the benefits so meaningful that it is worthwhile doing it.

PROTECTIVE AMULETS

Veteran feng shui practitioners begin each year by carefully making sure protective amulets and remedies are placed in the afflicted sectors of the home. Taoists are especially mindful of annual cures. Over the years, some of these cures have evolved into traditional rituals, which have become part of the cultural practices of the Chinese people. In some instances, cures can take on spiritual overtones.

There are many different kinds of amulet protectors.

Sometimes, incorporating powerful Sanskrit and Tibetan mantras or Chinese language invocations gives them added potency. The addition of red cinnabar or ground blue lapis powder can also make these cures more powerful. Wearing amulet symbols that contain powerful Kalachakra sand is also an excellent way of warding off bad vibes and keeping people with bad intentions towards you at bay.

Amulets and talismans can be worn on the body as rings, pendants or bracelets or they can be carried inside wallets or attached as special hangings on bags, placed above or flanking doorways and walls. Symbolic talismans protect our bodies while emblematic remedies protect our homes.

We also use auspicious objects to enhance the good fortune sectors of houses, thereby activating the lucky aspects of the year. The use of auspicious objects and celestial guardians has been part of many Asian cultures for many centuries. The tradition lives on in modern times simply because these talismans work. Besides, life has not become any safer. We continue to need protection against misfortune, premature death, illness and bad luck.

The Chinese have subscribed to the protection concept

for thousands of years. Archeological excavations attest to this as potteries from other eras and ancient antiquities show auspicious dragons, phoenixes, pi yaos, birds, fruits and flowers and a variety of objects. Today, these same symbols of good fortune continue to be as popular, featuring in many examples of contemporary and modern art. Feng shui symbols of good fortune can be in any style, art or design. They are effective when key elements of the symbolic cures or enhancing agents are incorporated.

BENEFICIAL ELEMENTS OF 2008

The coming year requires the elements of metal and fire. These two elements are missing in the Four Pillars Chart of 2008. This is one of the more serious revelations of the chart. Missing elements always suggest a lack of something and in the case of the current year, missing metal suggests a lack of strength and power. There is a lack of respect among people, leaders and nations – not a good indication. Missing fire indicates a shortage of intelligence and creativity. There is plenty of earth and wood energy, but the year is sorely lacking in metal and fire. The Earth Rat year needs metal and fire. These missing elements must be made available in order to enjoy success during the year.

MISSING SPRING

The year 2008 is also a year with a missing *Lap Chun*. Chinese New Year falls on February 7th and *Lap Chun* happens on February 4th. This is a year with an early spring, coupled with a missing *Lap Chun*, thereby suggesting that growth luck is sorely lacking.

According to master astrologists, the year also lacks fruiting and harvesting luck. These are severe afflictions that translate into a relatively barren year.

The chart does indicate plenty of earth element, which in 2008 stands for wealth luck. So the potential for creating wealth continues to exist. This indicates that earth luck is strong and those who can successfully use feng shui to improve their living space is sure to benefit.

GOOD INDICATIONS

Not everyone is in for a tough time. For instance, in 2008 those born under the animal signs of Dragon and Boar come into some special luck. The Dragon is blessed with the Earth Seal while the Heaven Seal visits the Boar. These two animal signs will experience some amazing good fortune in 2008. The Earth Seal brings the Dragon an earth-related project that will blossom into something particularly big, while the Boar will benefit from something totally unexpected coming his/her way in 2008.

The seals indicate potent authority from the stars and they bring special gifts to whichever animal signs play host to them. Those born in Dragon and Boar years should definitely carry or wear the words Earth *(Ti)* and Heaven *(Tien)* in Chinese on their bodies. Look for a golden pendant with these words. This is also a good year to activate the trinity of *Tien*, *Ti* and *Ren* in their respective directions of Southeast 1 for the Dragon and Northwest 3 for the Boar.

The Heaven and Earth seals also bring special energies to the sectors occupied by them during the year. They favour houses that face the SE1 and NW3 direction. There will be more on this in the feng shui sections of this book.

BORROWING LUCK

While some animal signs will be enjoying better luck than others, no single animal sign has a complete monopoly of good or bad luck in any given year. One's annual fortune always indicates both good and bad months, setbacks and triumphant moments. There are good periods and difficult times and the challenge is to map out a strategy for living.

Those going through a challenging year will discover they can insulate themselves so they don't feel the effects of a bad year too acutely. Those going through a robust year can likewise maximize their good fortune.

Chinese feng shui subscribes to the concept of "borrowing luck". This is a meaningful way to improve one's luck. When an animal sign has a rough year, it can borrow good luck from its astrological allies or secret friend. The animal signs are divided into four groups of three allies, and each sign also has a secret friend and a zodiac enemy.

One can strengthen one's luck by borrowing luck from allies and secret friends. One can also create the triangle of allies and secret friend within the house in an effort to light up the *Tien Ti Ren* of the house.

THE YEAR 2008

In 2008, indications suggest that difficulties loom large on several fronts. The almanac indicates plenty of rain, but it does not fall in the right places. The four seasons of Spring and Summer, Autumn and Winter come too early and this affects the fruiting of trees so there is less fruit to harvest. These metaphorical descriptions suggest an unbalanced year for those making a livelihood from agriculture.

The year is also one of clashing elements, with the heavenly stem being earth and the earthly branch being water. In the cycle of elements, earth destroys water. Clashing elements suggest disharmony and non-productivity. There are also more afflicted months in the coming year, and these require remedial cures, so close attention must focus on the ruling elements of each month.

THE FENG SHUI OF HOUSES

The energy of houses changes substantially each year. All houses should take account of these changes at the start of each new year. Updates ensure

the continuation of good feng shui, so we devote a section exclusively on the changing energy patterns of the coming year.

These are conveniently laid out so anyone can take the remedial actions required for their homes. Readers should take note of where to place cures and how to dissolve bad energy in afflicted sectors. Lucky enhancers that strengthen auspicious corners must also be noted. Make sure you are not only protected but that you can optimize your personal luck as well.

All houses are affected by the changing energy pattern. You may have benefited from good *chi* last year, but things can change in 2008. One example is the energy of the South, which in 2007 was very auspicious but which in 2008 gets hit by a number of afflictions

This year, North-facing houses enjoy good luck, as do East-facing houses, which receive good *chi* from the East and are supported by two generals at their back. The numbers of East and West make up the Ho Tu combination of 8/3 which brings good fortune to sons living here. Both the eldest and the youngest sons enjoy exceptional good fortune.

The big thing in 2008 is the glitter of gold. According to the almanac, this is a year when Golden Deities bring special good fortune. The year's chart also confirms the strong need for gold, so 2008 is a year to wear and display gold.

All advice in this book has been simplified. Advanced Chinese astrology and feng shui was never easier to practice even when you have had no previous experience of feng shui. This is one of twelve books, each based on an animal sign of the Chinese zodiac. Follow your personal forecasts and feng shui advised here and you will be optimizing your fortunes for the coming year.

Part One

- **THE DOG PERSONALITY**
  The Male Dog
  The Female Dog

- **COMPATIBILITY IN LOVE 2008**

THE DOG PERSONALITY

Check if you are a Dog person by using the following table. While doing that, also check the element of your heavenly stem to see what kind of Dog you are based on your year of birth.

Type of Dog (HS/EB)	Western Calendar Dates	Age	Kua Number Males	Kua Number Females	Heavenly Stem	Earthly Branch
Wood Dog	14 Feb 1934 to 3 Feb 1935	74	3 East Group	3 East Group	Yang Wood	Yang Earth
Fire Dog	2 Feb 1946 to 21 Jan 1947	62	9 East Group	6 West Group	Yang Fire	Yang Earth
Earth Dog	18 Feb 1958 to 7 Jan 1959	50	6 West Group	9 East Group	Yang Earth	Yang Earth
Metal Dog	6 Feb 1970 to 26 Jan 1971	38	3 East Group	3 East Group	Yang Metal	Yang Earth
Water Dog	25 Jan 1982 to 12 Feb 1983	26	9 East Group	6 West Group	Yang Water	Yang Earth
Wood Dog	10 Feb 1994 to 30 Jan 1995	14	6 West Group	9 East Group	Yang Wood	Yang Earth
Fire Dog	29 Jan 2006 to 17 Feb 2007	2	3 East Group	3 East Group	Yang Fire	Yang Earth

THE MALE DOG
THE FAITHFUL MALE DOG

Affectionate, faithful and loyal, the male of the Dog clan wears a sober, droopy countenance that reflects his pessimistic view of life. Here is a man who is cynical of the world. He whines and growls a lot, often about the multitude of wrongs, injustices and tragedies that befall mankind. Yet unless he is possessed of a strong dose of energy, he seldom does much about it.

He prefers to pontificate rather than do something to change the world, unless of course his element gives him the sorely needed courage and determination to do so. For the Dog gentleman does lack courage. Indeed, he is usually very risk averse. He is fearful and nervous, sometimes verging on paranoia. There is also a defeated look about him as if the burdens of the world are just too much to bear.

But the Dog male is fastidious and industrious. He does his work well and he can rise to great heights when sufficiently motivated. But this is more often the exception rather than the rule. This is because Dog men are rarely ambitious. They have no great yearning for that pot of gold at the end of the rainbow. They prefer to stay cocooned in their own self righteousness rather than join the hot pursuit for material success.

As soon as the Dog guy reaches a plateau in his career, he is quite content to spend his days researching, analyzing and criticizing the ills of mankind.

What is important to him? Justice! The environment! Human rights! Global warming! The rainforests of the world! All these are lofty and noble causes in today's world. Yet he is no visionary. He supports all of these causes from the armchair. And he will pontificate loudly and with eloquence to all who will listen. But will he stick his neck out, take risks for the cause, or die for his principles? Most certainly not! The Dog is not martyr material. He is more of an armchair critic!

But he is loyal and a great chum. He makes a devoted friend and a most affectionate companion. At a personal level he is the ultimate giver. In his personal relationships, he goes for the overkill and could quite easily overwhelm you with his acts of benevolence. He is appreciative of every little kindness; meticulously indebted for every small favour; and profuse in his gratitude.

He fears rejection with a passion and works at all his friendships. In any relationship, he is comfortable only when he is the giver and you the taker. But he needs loads of reassurance. If you are his girlfriend, he expects daily doses of tenderness, love and care. And you better keep every promise you make, because he is a hypersensitive soul and will read unintended slights into it even if you don't mean it.

THE WOOD MALE DOG

He is your best friend, your complete ally...the loyal chum... the faithful subordinate...the trustworthy partner. He can be relied upon absolutely. But the wood Dog abhors all things underhand. He has a natural aversion to lying and deceit and is usually unable to handle anything that contradicts his sense of morality. So he can be rather trying as a friend. Often his idealism is also dogmatic, making him doubly difficult to deal with.

Play fair and straight with him and he will reward you with long-term service and loyalty. This wood element Dog man often becomes a great success in later life. His will usually be a self-made success story, and the climb to the top will have been achieved through industry and conviction. It is unlikely that there would have been any subterfuge in his rise to the top. If you love him, be aware that he is a sensitive soul whose emotions can be quite surprisingly fragile, so treat him with much TLC.

THE FIRE MALE DOG

He is an uncompromising champion of the underdog. Well meaning and feisty, this fire male's idealism is often naïve and quixotic. To many more practical-minded people he can be rather tiresome. Yet he plods along unfazed by any cynicism or opposition he may encounter.

If and when he does give up, which is rare, he could be a broken man. The fire element's influence on the idealism of the Dog species can be deadly. Cool his passions by redirecting his energies to other causes. This is the best way to help him. Distract him by showing him the extent of the world's ills. Soothe his nerves by teasing him. The soft approach will work wonders. If you use harsh or strong language, the Dog male born of the fire element could well bite you, so do be careful around him!

THE EARTH MALE DOG

Michael Jackson is an earth Dog. Note how he makes brilliant music and gives stunning performances and then goes back to his sanctuary to recoup, doing his own thing hidden from the world's prying eyes. Look at his well meaning attempts to take on causes, to love children, and then see how he gets physically sick at the way his good intentions have been transformed into court suits against him!

A typical Dog tale indeed, one which is all too familiar when you examine an earth Dog man's life

chart. The sad thing is that the tendency to be misunderstood, and even be hounded for his good intentions continues well into his later life.

The earth Dog male requires solitude and peace but must not be left completely alone. When he lacks energy, he may be unable to bite back the way his Dog siblings can. It is possible that depression could set in and suicidal tendencies might take over. He is best when surrounded by those who genuinely care for him, as he thrives on encouragement and support. Love him and he can achieve great things.

THE METAL MALE DOG

This is the Dog that has the bite as well as the bark, and both can be equally painful! He is also the cleverest and most likely to succeed amongst his Dog siblings. The metal element tempers his persona with confidence and provides strength and perseverance, which enables him to marry idealism with practical action.

This Dog does not just talk. He also delivers. He does not whine; he growls. He is more Doberman than Daschund! But he is a great conversationalist and a superb mixer, moving easily in different social circles. He is less prone to bouts of depression and feelings of insecurity. If you love this guy, study him closely before making the big moves on him. You might decide he is too complicated for you, appearing to want you strong and weak at the same time. You need to be really patient to bring out the best in him.

THE WATER MALE DOG

He is affable and amiable, a real good friend. But his good intentions often border on being meddlesome and he is also frequently taken advantage of. He can be extremely handsome but often lacks courage and self esteem. Water Dogs tend to be impetuous. However, theirs is a false bravado, a courageous façade that is built on unstable ground. They need strong mates, women that can provide hidden support and strength.

If you can motivate him with a sense of self worth, he could well sparkle like a diamond, showing the world the best of his abilities and his charming personality. And then he becomes irresistible to watch. But do not withdraw your support. If you do, he could sink into a state of pessimism that could become his undoing. Dog people are such loyal friends that they too require the same kind of unstinting support. If they are betrayed, they seldom retaliate. Instead, they curl up and lick their wounds.

THE DOG LADY
THE GENEROUS DOG LADY

Agreeable, self-effacing and shy, the Dog female comes across quiet and introspective. Often a loner, always low profile and not terribly sociable, she drowns herself in work and is most comfortable when engaged in some charitable and noble purpose. She is generous, happily giving her time to those around her and dutifully fulfilling her chores, meticulously and with great fortitude.

The Dog woman is often naïve and innocent. Her world is wrapped around feel-good causes. To her, everything in life is serious, and there is little room for frivolous pursuits. She is neither materialistic nor very ambitious, being profoundly convinced that it is always advisable to be sober and careful, punctilious and correct. As a result, she seldom takes risks, and could even be said to be dull. Most of the time she appears anxious, especially when her in-bred pessimism makes her expect things to go wrong.

Despite the tendency at negativism however, the Dog lady is genuinely nice and touchingly candid and sincere. She makes the dearest friend possible and it would be difficult to find a more loyal or helpful ally. It is just that she can be so righteous in her view of the world. She takes great pride in being honest, faithful and proper, sometimes to the extent of being

holier than thou in her attitude, all of which can come across quite tiresome.

This lady is always worrying. She is often fearful and panicky. As a result, her whole attitude is one of anxiety. In any situation, you can depend on her to list out all the things that can go wrong. In the company of courageous and foolhardy people, she will tend to come across as that dreadful wet blanket. Yet she really cannot help herself.

She requires a great deal of emotional support and loads of tender loving care. Her heart is fragile and like marshmallow. On top of which she is often naïve in matters of love and romance. It is quite easy to take advantage of her easy, trusting nature. Often she knows it and will find herself a powerful mate to protect her from the big bad world. Think of the lovely Sophia Loren who lived under the protection of her powerful husband all her life. Emotionally, the Dog woman develops maturity late in life. And when she does, she might well devote herself to a cause that means a lot to her.

But the pessimism is more often than not all pervasive and many Dog women are unable to shake it off. As a result, many end up alone, as spinsters or favourite aunts! Unless she can find a mate who is prepared to invest massive doses of nurturing to strengthen her emotional make-up, those still alone late in life will find it hard to attract a mate.

THE WOOD FEMALE DOG

The wood lady Dog is profoundly affectionate, a real sweetheart, warm and caring and totally reliable. In fact she is so meticulously dependable you tend to think she is a pushover. But she truly is not. She is basically a giver, but she gives only to those she cares for and to causes she believes in. Hers is a strong conviction and she is almost never motivated by material gain, or by any covert or overt promises of recognition.

Dog women have to believe in what they are doing, and when they do, they bring to whatever project they are engaged in all their formidable doggedness to see things through. If a wood-born Dog lady loves you, consider yourself lucky. This is because her loyalty and support are legendary. The wonderful thing is that she supports without being clinging.

THE FIRE FEMALE DOG

Here is a modest and idealistic lady whose sincerity and earnestness usually endears her to many. Despite a pretty understated personality, she is often popular and sought after. The fire element imbues her with an eloquence that is persuasive and even influential, and when blessed with good luck, this brilliance makes her a compelling spokesperson for her favourite causes.

But when success eludes her, she can spiral into a dangerous vortex of addictive

Wood element energy radiates outwards in many directions, growing, rising and expanding. Wood has growth chi and is invaluable for fire element people

behaviour and suppressed rage. Depression can take hold unless she has someone she trusts close by. She feels things much too deeply and needs to lighten up. For this she needs the presence of a stronger person – someone who can be a mentor, a father figure, or an older female friend. Otherwise she could veer off course. When she has someone nearby however, the supportive energy, no matter how slight, is sufficient to help her pull herself together.

Earth element is in plentiful supply. Its energy spreads sideways. Earth combines with heaven energy to bring great good fortune.

Fire element's energy rises, moving ever upwards. It is an element that cannot be stored, but its brightness brings shining moments of fame and glory.

THE EARTH FEMALE DOG

She is reserved and secretive and is terribly uncomfortable with crowds. She usually avoids parties and heavy social occasions where she feels decidedly out of place and awkward. Not for her the cocktail type atmosphere where one has to resolutely work through a sea of unfamiliar faces. The earth lady Dog is hypersensitive and her view of the world is coloured by a deep-seated conviction that everything will always go wrong. She is convinced that if anyone wants to make friends with her, it will be for some ulterior motive. Alas, because she believes these things so strongly, things usually do go wrong for her, and fair weather friends do surround her.

What she needs is to attend a course in positive thinking or in building self esteem. However, she does often make an effort to be adaptable and she usually responds positively to someone strong and loving. There is no danger of her being a clinging sort however, and this makes it easier for her to attract someone to her side.

THE METAL FEMALE DOG

This lady has a bark and a bite! She is a grande dame with the confidence to accomplish great things... climb Mount Fuji, find a cure for Aids, revolutionize the education system... anything

Metal is anything made of brass, gold or other metals. In 2008 there is an astrological shortage of metal.

which catches her imagination and her strong sense of social responsibility.

The metal element adds wonderful sparkle to her idealism and is usually sufficient to spur her to action. It is as if she receives continuous boosts of energy. She harnesses her deep passion in her interests incredibly well, making her an effective leader when it comes to her favourite charitable causes. She is not money-minded for her own sake, thus would never be the cutthroat, ruthless sort in business. But cross her and her bite could be worse than her bark.

She is choosy but loyal and will growl her way into anyone's heart. But take care, she is not to be trifled with. Do not play with her feelings and never try to double cross her. She is tenacious at getting her own back. This lady bites!

THE WATER FEMALE DOG

She is quite terrifically beautiful with a slight air of aloofness that says it all. She is the hardest of the Dogs to get to know and is more aware of her pedigree than the other element dogs. She can be aggressive but not vicious or malevolent. Her bark is worse than her bite.

As a friend she is as loyal as all Dogs, but it is not easy getting close to her. She has an instinctive internalized spirit of self preservation which she rarely lets down, and unless she has researched you, chances are she will keep you at arms length. But break through and she will overwhelm you with affection. Like her Dog sisters, her loyalty can be amazingly firm and resolute but it is two way thing. She also has high expectations of those close to her. Let her down and she could turn away. So with her, one really needs to stay completely supportive.

Water can be a flow or an accumulation. When correctly harnessed, water brings wealth.

Part One

• **COMPATIBILITY IN LOVE 2008**

DOG / RAT

MISMATCHED ENERGIES MAKE 2008 HARD FOR THESE TWO

the year 2008 brings very different *chi* to the Dog and to the Rat so this couple does not have it easy. Their energies are out of sync this year. The Rat is blessed with pure yang power from heaven, while the Dog has to suffer through a year of weak and sickly energy. The illness star brings vulnerability to the environmental forces making it hard for the Dog to keep up with the high flying Rat. So while one is strong and vigourous the other is feeling miserable and weak.

In this situation, much depends on the Rat's feelings, which for the most time is genuine. The problem with Rat is that he/she is easily distracted this year. These are two animal signs whose initial feelings are loving, and in good times they

are gentle and affectionate with each other; but in 2008 the year is not kind to the Dog. There are aches and pains and plenty of ailments to cope with. What the Dog needs is lots of tender loving care, but the Rat's attention is focused in other directions and becomes a rather detached sort of partner, doing his/her own thing. Perhaps the problem is that he/she is simply too busy pursuing high flying goals and craving for upward social mobility. As a result, the relationship between the two suffers hugely.

It is not that the Rat is selfish, only that as the year progresses or as the relationship gets closer much of the gloss in the coupling disappears and the Rat finds the relationship unexciting and uninspiring. Unfortunately both then discover they have too little in common to make things work so once the magic of loving flies out the window they will separate. All that's left is a feeling of emptiness. This year is not conducive to them discovering beauty in each other so they need to work hard at staying together.

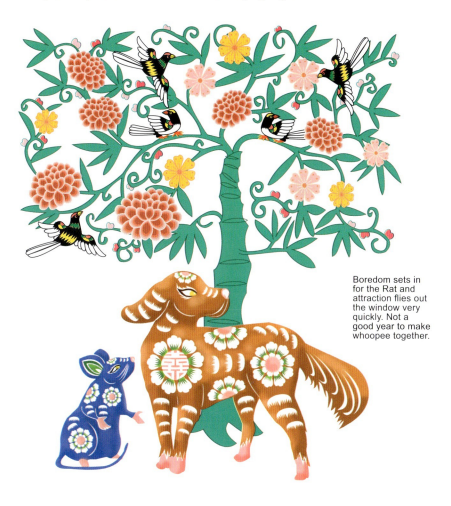

Boredom sets in for the Rat and attraction flies out the window very quickly. Not a good year to make whoopee together.

DOG / OX

♥ ♥ ♥ ♥

DISTRACTIONS IN AN OTHERWISE FUN-FILLED YEAR

The Ox and Dog can look forward to a happy time in 2008 when love is in the air and romance has a chance to blossom. These two have a special affinity brought about by the similarity of their elements – both being earth people based on their astrological signs, and in 2008 they also benefit from the Ox's peach blossom luck. The main thing causing an obstacle to their happiness is the Dog's weak energy and the curse of the illness star.

The Dog is feeling poorly this year and despite everything this does cause a certain amount of stress for this couple. Many well laid plans for holidays, projects and outings get stymied as a result of the differences in energy levels of this pair. This is a situation where unbalanced *chi* energies work against them, causing intolerance and a certain frustration to set in. The year does not appear to be very kind to the Dog in this respect and it spills over into his/her relationship luck.

A certain amount of resentment could set in if the Ox does not demonstrate sufficient patience, love and support. Going through a year when one succumbs easily to illness cannot be easy. And when your lover shows a lack of understanding, it can become a big bone of contention. It is also possible that other pressures set in for the Dog that cause mental afflictions and the Ox finds it difficult to be understanding and patient.

Despite this, this pair are likely to pull through the year's afflictions. This is because there are happiness occasions. Despite the dogmatic and seemingly uncaring Ox irking the normally easy-going Dog, this is a couple whose loyalty for each other holds them together. They have the power and ability to create happy times that on balance could make this pairing work. If they can work their obstacles through the year, the pair should stay together.

This relationship may be strained in 2008 due to Dog's poor luck, but their underlying compatibility will see them get through the year just fine.

WELL BALANCED LUCK BRING THESE TWO CLOSER

For these astrological allies, 2008 brings a time of matching strength and *chi* energy. These two will take strength from each other and they could also grow stronger as a couple.

The year ahead is a good time to strengthen their commitment to each other. The Dog has to endure the negative afflictions associated with illness vibes while the Tiger is feeling romantic and passionate. In spite of this however, the energy levels of these two animal signs are the same and they both enjoy the star of Small Luck which suggests that in all the small things, the tiny situations that make up the sum total of living, these two will enjoy a smooth year. This is the kind of energy conducive to people falling in love and staying in love.

This match works because the Dog understands the Tiger's nature completely, and the vibes of 2008 ensure that the Dog personality will stay indulgent and caring towards the Tiger. Meanwhile, the Tiger is most appreciative of the Dog's generosity of spirit, patience and kind nature. Neither side will be floored in any way in the presence of any setbacks. The Dog's illness star affliction will also not come between them at all. Their mutual respect of each other makes the match last. Their affinity is obvious and they can overcome anything.

The long term outlook for this pair looks most promising indeed. They are in full simpatico with each other. The future together looks bright and in good times or bad, their astrological connections will always hold them together.

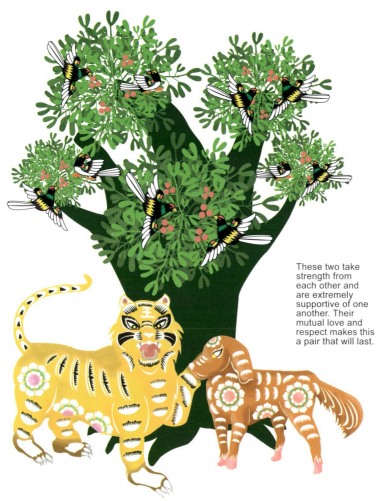

These two take strength from each other and are extremely supportive of one another. Their mutual love and respect makes this a pair that will last.

♥ ♥ ♥ ♥

RABBIT ASSISTS DOG IN 2008

t he Rabbit and Dog are considered a particularly well-matched pair in the Chinese zodiac. So this union is already on a steady footing as dictated by the wishes of heaven. Not only will you get on naturally well with each other, you can prop and support each other up endlessly without feeling used or taken advantage of. This can only strengthen your relationship since both sides are only too willing to help each other out. This is an auspicious coupling as there is much common ground, and spiritually both are attuned to each other's unsaid needs.

However in 2008, the Rabbit will have to play the dominant role and assist the Dog more than usual, as the Dog suffers from illness and exhaustion woes.

The Dog will tend to get sick easily and enjoys small doses of luck only. There is also the possibility of accidents and minor irritations that seem to beset the poor Dog throughout the year.

The Dog should display the Medicine Buddha or the Kuan Yin statue in gold; or wear a Medicine Buddha bracelet to safeguard against illness all through the year. The Dog's 24 mountain star in 2008 is the star of Small Luck which needs to be expanded and enhanced. With the Rabbit for a life partner, there will be joyous occasions, so the pairing of Dog with Rabbit is auspicious for the Dog.

Both can attain much satisfaction, as there is great rapport between them. This encourages both to strive to greater heights, with the laudable intention of pleasing each other. Passion and feelings will grow intense and it is up to both parties whether to allow them to sizzle or let them explode. Whatever the outcome, both will demonstrate love and affection and this coupling can be viewed as a formidable partnership that is not easily shaken. If both enter business, then it is even better as each will inspire the other.

Dog and Rabbit can make a formidable partnership both in love and business. They have great rapport with each other and are spiritually attuned to each other's needs.

DRAGON WILL HAVE UPPER HAND IN RELATIONSHIP

traditionally the Dragon and Dog makes for the worst possible pairing and old folks always warn against such a union. In olden days, no matchmaker worth her salt would ever suggest a Dragon be betrothed to a Dog or vice versa.

The Dog suffers from the effects of the illness star this year, so it is vulnerable to a myriad of health issues. The Dog must display the Medicine Buddha in gold or wear the Medicine Buddha bracelet to ward off the negativity of the illness star. Its Small Auspicious star is a big consolation as it brings many small but joyous occasions to the home. So if the Dragon is staying with a Dog, then it can look forward to plenty of warm homecomings though it may have to play nursemaid now and then!

Generally this is an uneven, unexciting and uninteresting year for both should they live together as couple. The Dragon gets the upper hand most of the time and is seen to be the one in control especially when it receives large income or revenue from various sources.

Communication between these two may be hard as both sides seem to prefer giving orders rather than listening to what the other has to say! Animosity can set in, as even a couple can get jealous of each other. Beware not to allow frustrations and lingering resentment to build up or else the relationship has little chance of survival into 2009.

These natural adversaries of the zodiac will find it difficult to get through 2008 as a couple.

DOG / SNAKE

DIVERGING INTERESTS, MAY DRIFT APART IN 2008

this match is by no means perfect, and in 2008 this couple will encounter many mountains to climb. If married or going steady, the Snake and Dog may find themselves stuck in a rut and feeling like they have passed the 'use by' date. This is the year to revive the old flames as some embers are still smoldering, so don't let them get extinguished if you want the union to last.

If you care for your partner, it is time to let it be known as sometimes two people get too accustomed with each other and begin to take each other for granted. You two seem compatible enough to try and make a go of it, but sometimes you prefer to let things take their course, resulting in a gradual drifting apart, though usually one of you comes to your senses and quickly patches things up before the rot sets in.

The earth element of the Dog exhausts the fire element of the Snake, while the Snake's fire produces the Dog's earth. In this relationship, it will tend to be the Snake that supports the Dog. And for the longevity of the coupling, it is better this way.

The Dog is prone to illness and accidents this year so the Snake who seems fit as a fiddle may have to play nursemaid often. As long as it is not serious, the Snake is more than happy to indulge and pander to the whims of the Dog, who has a tendency to whine once too often this year. The Dog enjoys Small Auspicious luck which results in many small but joyful occasions at home, so the two of them can at least look forward to some delightful nights in.

Try to find common ground when differences arise; you have come far enough not to throw the towel in at this point. As a couple, you may find many occasions there is a clash of wills. It is not easy but since it is only between the two of you, there is no harm in giving in. Communication may be a problem, so it is advisable not to bottle everything inside; it is better to talk it out with each other. This is the best way of overcoming important differences. Yours is a relationship that has the potential to bring out the best in each other, so it is worthwhile putting in the effort. Once you stop talking, you run a real risk of drifting apart.

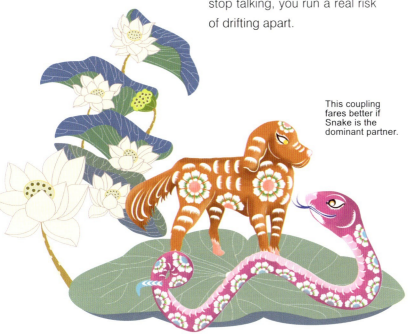

This coupling fares better if Snake is the dominant partner.

DOG / HORSE

♥ ♥ ♥ ♥

COMPATIBILITY BRINGS SOME BRILLIANT DAYS

The Horse and Dog are astrological allies who enjoy a natural affinity with each other. They make a loving and caring pair as both have temperaments that bring out the best in each other. Each knows by instinct the emotional moods of the other and they show their love in many endearing ways.

Even after decades of marriage, this is a pair who can still spring pleasant surprises on each other. This reveals good things about the union as their love can really withstand the tests of time. Like fine wine, the pair grows more attuned to each other as the years roll by and their relationship simply improves with age!

While this is a poor year for the Horse, with the Dog in tow providing support and luck, it can survive 2008 in one piece. The only fly in the ointment is the Dog's weak health as it may succumb to the effects of the illness star. Of course in unity there is strength and love can conquer all no matter what the afflictions or tribulations. Problems are indeed superficial in the face of real commitment between two people who have so much affinity with each other.

The Dog will bring luck in small and gentle ways to the Horse this year, and this pair can expect many happy events at home, which although may not be overly momentous will certainly be memorable. The

Horse and Dog can cuddle up nicely, enjoying the comfort of home and hearth together. Love is in the air and both find immense solace and comfort in each other's arms and company. When the world seems cruel to the Horse, it knows where to go for the greenest pastures!

Horse and Dog enjoy a great natural affinity and in 2008 will find comfort and solace in each other's arms.

DOG / SHEEP

♥ ♥ ♥ ♥

COMMUNICATING ON THE SAME WAVELENGTH

this is considered an average combination, neither great nor terrible. But if they play their cards right and are in love, then chances of getting married are good. If already hitched, this year can take them to a new level of appreciation for each other.

This pair should enjoy a relatively harmonious year with no major disruptions as there is good affinity in their *chi* energies. They can communicate on the same wavelength as there is much common ground. Indeed there is more to link them together than pull them apart. Theirs is not the ideal partnership, but they get on with a great start this year. All they need do is maintain the momentum and not let jealousy get in the way. The Dog seems more flirtatious than ever and seems quite receptive to newfound attention and flattery from outside sources.

The Dog enjoys the bounty of the Small Luck star, which brings delightful and joyous occasions. The Dog will benefit much from this lucky star and his/her partner will also share the reflected glory. In fact, the Sheep who does not have the same kind of luck will benefit from a liaison with the Dog, as this will give Sheep a much needed boost in 2008. Unfortunately, the Dog, while enjoying good money luck, could see health issues crop up periodically. The Sheep's protective nature will make the Dog feel loved and comforted during ill times, which will sweeten things between the two.

This is a year when fortune comes from the divine as well as from earthly sources and promises much in terms of personal satisfaction. A few schemes remain castles in the air but a few should come to fruition, fuelling their amour even more. When one partner is well off and successful, the other can always be called upon to help out.

Dog and Sheep make a loving pair who are sympatico with each other. 2008 favours this pairing and they could emerge even stronger as a couple.

DOG / MONKEY

SMALL OBSTACLES SHOULD NOT DETER THIS PAIR

This pair will face some obstacles and may have to prove how far their love can go this year. It's not a walk in the park but not climbing Mount Everest either. All things can come to a satisfactory conclusion if both put their heads together and collude for a common aim.

The focus is on the Dog whose fidelity may be in doubt more than once this year. The Dog suffers from the illness star and when hit with the sniffles, may make a big fuss for the sake of attention. If Dog perceives he/she is getting less than expected, then he/she could well use this as an excuse to look elsewhere. Dog seems to pick on Monkey at the drop of a hat and is very demanding and cranky. At times, Dog may seem unreasonable, insisting on being pampered incessantly. Monkey is very ardent in love and as long as it can pander to the whims and fancies of Dog, then he/she should be able to cling onto the driver's seat.

But Dog's big advantage this year is that he/she enjoys the Small Auspicious star so there are happy occasions to be enjoyed at home. If Dog and Monkey are a couple, then both should be able to enjoy these joyous occasions right in the comfort of their own home. This may well prove to be the turning point as both may discover they have much in common and that they enjoy each other's company too much for them to let go.

Judgments on both sides may occasionally occur but the Monkey is in a forgiving mood even though it may be flirtatious too. But while the Dog can be genuine, it can also be the cause of heartache and worries. They seem to have differing temperaments but luck may be on the side of the Monkey as it enjoys the patronage of the Golden Deities. This star is very significant as it has the power to bestow support and auspiciousness to everyone in the Monkey's household. Coupled with the Dog's Small

Auspicious star, they can create magical ambiances in the serenity and safety of their 'castle'. If the two realize they have a good thing going then there is no reason to look elsewhere.

Health and money-wise, both Monkey and Dog are doing respectably, so that is another worry obliterated. With no financial woes or major issues, there is every reason for this relationship to work to everyone's satisfaction.

These two have differing temperaments but this pairing can work with some effort from both sides.

PROBLEMS ROB THIS PAIR OF THEIR LUSTRE IN 2008

This less than ideal pairing are beset with love problems and many office issues get taken home. This will not be a memorable year as there are too many obstacles that may leave a lingering bitter aftertaste even after the year is over.

The Rooster is very competitive, aggressive and unsympathetic, so may appear unsympathetic should the Dog fall ill as it is under the aegis of the illness star. Sure the Rooster is genuinely concerned, but actions rarely follow sympathetic sentiments. The Rooster will be a pain during 2008 incessantly nagging the Dog on various matters.

The Rooster, always the more dominant personality, becomes extra authoritative, status conscious and can even be seen as a something of a bully in 2008. Blame it on the Two Generals star under which it falls, as this star pushes the Rooster to be more assertive and power hungry. This works very well in the office as such confidence can help in the climb up the corporate ladder, but such bravado may not work so well in bedroom.

The Rooster is more outwardly successful than the Dog this year, but this does not mean Rooster will bankroll Dog. If Dog is expecting hand-outs, he/she may be barking up the wrong tree. The Rooster, despite a healthy cash flow, will want to dictate how and where the money goes, which may not be what the Dog expects.

Both however can look forward to some happy moments together at home, as the Dog enjoys the Small Auspicious star, which brings joy to the household. These two have strong minds and powerful intellects and when they are at odds with each other, they can bring out the worst in each other. This love affair will be punctuated with outbursts of anger and recriminations.

In 2008 the Rooster is quick to anger while the Dog feels physically weak. When there is strife, it is a good idea for one to go on holiday or move back to his/her own family home temporarily. Distance can lend some soothing medication while feelings and expressions of anger do little good.

A problematic year for this pairing, making this coupling one punctuated by outbursts of anger and irritation. Rooster has to tone down for this relationship to work.

PERSONAL GROWTH AMID CHALLENGES IN 2008

This pair according to traditional astrology is not the perfect choice for matchmakers. They feel and care strongly for each other, yet feel something holding them back. What each does fails to achieve the desired effect with the other. Little frustrations strung together can strain even the strongest of relationships and this is something two Dogs do not have – a strong relationship. Dog people can be very loyal to their friends, but with lovers it can sometimes be another story.

2008 is fraught with little mountains to scale and raging rivers to cross. They yearn for personal growth and look towards romance, but both are under the illness star, which can play havoc with their love and personal lives. If there is a bug doing the rounds, one or both are bound to catch the sniffles. With two Dogs sharing the same fate, the illness star can wield stronger power and sickness can be a major source of worry. If two Dogs are staying in the same house, it behoves them to install feng shui cures to counter their illness woes. They should display the Medicine Buddha in gold, or a Wu Lou health gourd made of metal. They can also each wear the Medicine Buddha bracelet as this is the best way to keep illness at bay.

A little goes a long way, more so when there are many reasons to stay healthy to enjoy the glad tidings of the Small Auspicious star, which the Dog enjoys this year. This lucky star brings happy occasions into their house. They can stay at home and enjoy the comforts it provides and be perfectly content. The Small Luck star can also denote the arrival of a child or the marriage of someone dear.

It is a good idea to host small parties and gatherings at home. Guests and their energy will activate the Small Auspicious star and suppress the effects of the illness star. When there is a rush of yang energy in the home, the illness star gets reduced. This helps the relationship, as two Dogs getting sick make a miserable pair.

There is money to be made and this can sweeten the relationship. When money worries are removed from the love equation, life gets easier and passion has room to intensify. While Dogs may think prosperity means more money, they should also consider the other possibility; spiritual progress. If they become more spiritual and charitable, they may well realize this is their road to personal growth.

Two Dogs are not the best match and may find 2008 strenuous on their relationship.

DOG / BOAR

♥ ♥ ♥ ♥

FINANCIAL SUCCESS DRAW THEM CLOSE IN 2008

these two have a natural affinity that seems blessed by the heavens in 2008. Their instant rapport is bewitching and easily transcends the grinds and pitfalls of living together. They have differing personalities and hardly seem to have much in common, yet they can communicate far more openly than most couples with shared interests. As they say, opposites attract! They are well-grounded individuals with their feet firmly planted on terra firma. There is little that can upset them and despite many tempting offers from others, these two remain faithful to each other in 2008.

Unfortunately, one of the things they share this year is sickness as both fall under the illness star. They will have to nurse each other, but this is a role both should enjoy, since looking after the ailing partner is taken seriously and not seen as a chore. To ward off the ill effects from this star, they should display Medicine Buddha in their home, or the Wu Lou. Since both have the illness star to contend with, the effects can be seriously compounded as the yin effect is dramatically increased.

They must stay fit as a fiddle to enjoy what the year brings them. The Dog has the Small Auspicious star which brings joy and prosperity while the Boar receives the blessings from the Heaven Seal star which showers more glad tidings and support from heavenly sources.

With two favourable stars shining down on them, their

home should be a haven of happiness. To reinforce their quota of good luck, they should throw more parties and host dinners regularly to increase the yang energy of their home and eradicate any lurking bad *chi*.

They complement each other and the presence of one can only inspire the other to perform even better. Yet there are scant traces of jealousy. Their magnanimous mood extends to family and friends as their generosity is taken to new heights this year.

An air of triumph pervades their home and there are few reasons to quarrel and many reasons to celebrate. This glow of happiness is made possible as one is willing to play second fiddle to the other. There are no hard and fast rules about who is bringing in the bacon or who should pay which bills, so their life moves smoothly without any timetable or rules, and it works for them!

A couple that easily transcends the grinds and pitfalls of living together. This pairing is one that can weather any obstacles and last a long time.

Part Two

- **OUTLOOK & LUCK OF THE DOG IN 2008**

- **PERSONAL HOROSCOPE PLANNER FOR 2008**
  The Dog's Luck in Each Month of the Year

the following year could be something of a challenge for the Dog, who will be plagued by illness, poor health, accidents and mishaps. Elderly Dogs should ensure they have ample longevity symbols around them. Wearing the Medicine Buddha bracelet is a powerful talisman against illness energies, as is displaying the Medicine Buddha prominently in your home. Avoid sleeping in a Northwest bedroom this year. If you have to, have a brass wu lou by your bedside. You are prone to exhaustion and could feel physically weaker than your usual bounding self, which could be frustrating when there's so much you want to get done. You can handle a lot, you just need to recognize when to take a break!

On the upside, Dogs enjoy the star of Small Auspicious, which brings joyful occasions into your personal life. There are happy occasions to enjoy with the family, and Dogs who are parents will particularly enjoy this role this year. Though 2008 is not a year where big battles are won or great victories achieved, the small things are just as important as they keep you sane in an otherwise arduous and tiring year. *Hei See* occasions are in the charts; you could have a wedding, birth

Eight Immortal
Wu Lou

of a new baby, or big birthday in the family to celebrate this year. Dogs who celebrate such events can further boost their luck this year.

Work-wise you do average. Although your work is recognized, you may feel you're not getting the recognition you deserve. Persevere and your efforts will deliver results soon enough, but you may have to wait till third quarter before things really begin to happen for you. Wealth-wise there is money to be made, but this will not be blow-the-mind-away money. But if you plan carefully you could build up a sizeable kitty or holiday fund for end of the year. Take a well-deserved vacation with the family this year – make it meaningful and don't scrimp too much.

Dogs who are married or with a long-term partner could find themselves leaning on their better halves this year. Your partner provides tremendous support so don't hesitate to go for help if you need. Two heads are better than one, so if you have a confidante to confide in, don't shy away make the most of it!

When you're unsure, resist the urge to do the impulsive thing. Think things through. Strategize. There's no need to act immediately, or give an answer directly. Use time to plan before you speak and act. Making important decisions on impulse could cause you to regret this year.

The year begins well with your energy levels still up from last year. February and March are lucky for you, so plan important events during these months. April brings some danger of money loss, so avoid speculation and risky investments then. May brings plenty of opportunities as well as helpful people into your life. This is when your past networking efforts will lead to some positive results.

Beware June when illness and misfortune hits you hard; lay low and don't take any risks. Look after your health as well as personal safety. September is another month when you could get really sick. Don't take health issues lightly this year. By October you will feel your luck start to change for the better, and the rest of the year will likely be infinitely better than the first part.

For Dogs, the best advice this year is to pace yourself. You have overall good luck but could find yourself slowed down by waning energy, ill health and other mishaps. If you look after yourself, this will not be a bad year at all.

Love luck is particularly good though you prefer relationships to be serious than casual dating. Single Dogs looking for a mate should keep this in mind because superficial dating could play havoc with your emotions and leave you feeling dissatisfied and disturbed.

Young Dogs will find this a good year for study and learning, and will not lack initiative. Those who find a suitable mentor can leapfrog their mates in the results league.

The only area the Dog needs to worry about this year is health, so remember to exercise, watch your diet, get enough rest and eliminate all poison arrows, physical or mental, from your life.

Part Two

- **PERSONAL HOROSCOPE PLANNER FOR 2008**

1ST MONTH
FEBRUARY 4TH - MARCH 5TH 2008

A BUSY TIME

The Dog wags in the New Year with plenty on its plate so cannot complain about not having enough to do! You are quite inspired to get everything done on time as you are up and raring to go as if up for lost time. The new year puts you in a positive mood and you are eager to get started. However, you may suffer from flagging energy which is a double whammy as you strive to finish projects yet may be physically or mentally exhausted.

You need friends, allies and experts to help you! Once you realize you cannot hope to get everything done on your own, you should feel better. You enjoy minor prosperity this month so can hope to make some dough. Your best bet is to let things run their course and not push your limited luck. Don't take risks or you may only be exposing yourself to more tension and troubles!

CAREER
BUSY

You are busy as a bee this month but this is good as you feel like working hard. Your popularity level is high. You are well liked and people in high places notice the effort you have put in lately, so this augurs well.

Delivering good results is a cinch for you these days though some stress may be encountered since you seem to be battling deadlines incessantly. Luckily it is not a matter of banging your head against a brick wall; you somehow manage to triumph and complete tasks even at the last minute!

If you are feeling under the weather due to mounting pressures, cancel weekend appointments and use them to chill out. The R & R will do you a world of good. Recharging is necessary or you will get burnt out.

Be considerate as you climb the corporate ladder; it is possible to get what you want without trampling on others! You are in dire need of allies and cannot afford adding more enemies to your life. Take time to sit down, detach yourself from the everyday tension and organize yourself mentally. Forcing yourself to take stock of what is going on will help you in the long run.

BUSINESS
NETWORKING NEEDED

Those in public relations and advertising do particularly well this month as the stars favour the media, publicity and events. Even if you are not involved in this line, it augurs well to network and socialize actively as many valuable contacts can be had during such times. You may even land one or two contracts unexpectedly simply by being in the right place at the right time! So you have little to lose but your evening hours and quite likely plenty to gain!

You are good with words this month so clinching a deal seems easier than before as you appear convincing and enthusiastic during presentations and sales pitches. Your money luck is limited so don't expect anything mind-blowing! If you can close some small deals, you should be grateful! But what you can do now is lay the foundations for future expansion and success which is just as vital, as your wealth luck crystallizes next month and better things are on the way.

If you insist on taking risks, make sure they are calculated ones with some chance of success as you simply cannot trust blind faith now. Be careful of hurtling headlong into things you will regret later. Think before you act and especially before you sign; run the contract through your lawyer first! You may need to consciously slow down as your mind seems to be working overtime and not all ideas you have now are that brilliant, so don't be overly ambitious.

ROMANCE
GOOD

A promising and generally happy month for Dogs keen on the opposite sex! If you are in the mood for love, then you are in for some thrills.

Things can happen pretty fast on the romantic front so enjoy life and go with the flow. The tides of romance won't lead you astray!

Single Dogs may meet someone very interesting who catches your eye this month. Love hangs so heavy in the air that going steady, getting engaged or even getting married are on the cards.

If you are just on the first flush of romance, it is a good time to go on a romantic holiday with your special someone. You are bound to have a jolly passionate time! While your relationship may be fuelled by passion and drama, you should also make the most of this magical time to get to know the person better.

Married Dogs should resist the urge to be unfaithful and that applies to those who are engaged or about to do so. Fooling around will come to a bad end, so don't succumb to a temporary weakness.

FAMILY
HECTIC

Your home is hardly a haven of peace and calm this month. There are so many things going on you may even think your office is quieter! You are loaded with responsibilities and things you feel are not due to your making yet you seem to be the only one doing all the running, heaving and puffing! No wonder your temper is not so sanguine!

Talk to your family; it may well be that at other times you were the one who insisted on all the extra workload and your siblings, spouse and relatives are now taking you for granted. This is a good time to talk things out. Don't bottle everything up inside; you will be much happier if you say what you feel rather than expect others to be mind readers.

Now is a good time to get to know each individual family member better. You can also re-connect with siblings you have fallen out with; remember, blood is thicker than water.

If married, you can get closer to a son or daughter who seems to be distant of late. All you need is make a little effort and you will set the ball in motion. Relationships go well this month and this applies to your professional career, family members and even outsiders.

EDUCATION
EXCELLENT

Younger Dogs getting an education are in for an excellent time. Most things go your way and no one is raining on your parade this month. Your hard work is recognized and nothing is too tough.

The carp successfully jumping over the Dragon Gate indicates successfully passing your exams and starting a fruitful career.

If studies are what you wish to excel in, this is when you will be amply rewarded. All you need is some ordinary effort, which is easy as pie since so much is already in place! You have the potential to do very well in exams as well as in your usual studies this month, so you can pat yourself on the back.

Your personality proves to be another asset and will take you far. Teachers warm towards you and classmates think you are, well, top dog! A good time to set high standards for yourself. You can aim for a higher level with greater chances than ever of succeeding.

2ND MONTH
MARCH 6TH - APRIL 4TH 2008

WEALTH & PROSPERITY

The Prosperity Star and its companion the Fortune Star have flown into your chart. This is an extremely potent combination, so make the most of it while you can. Expect extraordinary money-making opportunities to flow into your life. You are also in a good position to take full advantage of them.

This is also a great time to plan for the big things in life, like marriage, moving house, changing job or signing new deals. Your karma is in full swing and you seem to reach full circle, but to complete it, you should do some charity work or donate to worthwhile causes. The more you give, the more you receive.

CAREER
EXCELLENT CAREER LUCK

Career luck is excellent and everything goes smoothly according to plan. Even if there are minor hiccups, you are totally unfazed as you are able to see the bigger picture.

You can get promoted, enjoy a raise or be given extra perks like car, expense account or even a PA. More importantly, you get to do what you really like and when your work is recognized, you may even feel bashful as you hardly felt like you were slaving away!

There are opportunities to get close to the boss. Your social skills and external contacts also come in handy. This is the time to put in that extra effort as rewards are out of proportion to what you put in. If you were planning to leapfrog into management or directorship, now is your chance.

Don't follow the herd like a pack dog. Assert and show off some leadership qualities if you want to be seen as a leader.

Monkey on a swift running horse means your career is on a fast track.

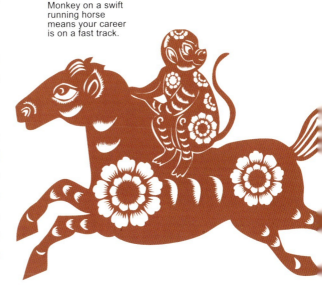

Nine coins on a red string bring excellent profits and continued success in business.

BUSINESS
GREAT

Great month for Dogs in business. All those sleepless nights wondering if you made the right decisions will now come to an end as you realize there was no cause to worry. Recently made decisions will bear fruit and even if they fail to do so, your luck is so strong there are many more opportunities to augment your wealth. As one window closes, two new ones open!

This is a good time to invest, so you can take some risks. You are in line for some form of windfall, so think positive as the more good luck you expect, the more such glad tidings will flow into your life. Projects get started earlier than expected and even better, get completed ahead of schedule!

This is also a fortuitous time to invest in research and development as something from this department will greatly benefit you.

ROMANCE
DON'T GET TOO SERIOUS

Unlike last month, love is more about the head than the heart. This is not so bad as you now prefer to see the medium to long term possibilities rather than instant gratification! You are concerned about where the relationship is taking you in the foreseeable future rather than what is happening at this moment.

Of course this attitude may cause passion to fly out the window somewhat and your sweetheart cannot be too pleased. Don't get too serious or academic if you want to keep the magic alive!

Some marital strife for married Dogs may occur; best is heart-to-heart discussions with your spouse to sort out differences. These may involve finances and may require the two of you to decide who is responsible for what! Most relationships and marriages are unequal in the sense you may be dominant or submissive. There is absolutely nothing wrong in being one or the other! Make your choice and your partner will follow suit.

FAMILY
FULFILLING

Domestic life on the home front is particularly fulfilling and you feel especially close to those who are already dear and near. If you don't have strong ties with the family, you will feel the need to build them. This is a good month to develop new relationships or repair damaged ones. The stars are in favour of domestic bliss, so anything connected with family will result in happy times.

If you have spare cash, take the family for a nice holiday. Even weekend treats and outings to shopping malls will end up with joyous memories that stay for ages. They will also be really delighted and appreciative if you buy them gifts!

The Northwest of your home is very auspicious this month, so some redecorating will result in strengthening the already powerful *chi*. If you are the patriarch of the house, you will enjoy increased influence as the rest simply adore and appreciate your wisdom.

This auspicious plant of peony and ling zhi means longevity and nobility without limit.

EDUCATION
AUSPICIOUS

Dogs in the process of being educated will enjoy an auspicious month. The stars shine down on you, so use this lucky period to show how talented you are!

It is easy to make your mark in the classroom so you might as well leave an indelibly good impression! Teachers favour you so this is the best time to get to know them better. No harm in being teacher's pet rather than someone they dread!

Your learning rate goes up and your powers of retention are extremely strong. You absorb knowledge like a sponge. If you were not that hot on studies previously, now is the time to steer yourself to love learning which of course is why you are there in the first place. If you are already a good scholar, you will do well without even trying. Aim high and you will be pleasantly amazed how high you can go!

3RD MONTH
APRIL 5TH - MAY 5TH 2008

DANGER OF ROBBERY

After the relative highs of last month come the relative lows. While bad luck comes whether you like it or not, you still have the power to soften the blows! So by the end of the month you will be relieved to know you managed to get off better than expected.

It is all about money this month, or rather the lack of it! Cash flow may be strained as unexpected expenses crop up. There is also possibility of losing money, either through carelessness, bad investment or getting robbed. Be careful where you go. Keep your eyes peeled for strangers hanging nearby. Keep an eye on your handbag and have your car keys ready in hand rather than waste time fumbling and searching for them in lonely car parks. Put personal safety first. However, in the same breath you also have the luck to make some money as well.

Accept small losses and be careful if involved in business. Make sure you are not exposed as you are vulnerable right now and can lose big money. The Robbery Star afflicts you so you must think on your feet.

CAREER
TOUGH

You may have enemies in the ranks and they can plot against you. Things are tough if the lines are not clear cut; you may not know who is on your side and who is secretly jealous of you and wish you ill. Those who seem friendly and courteous may be the culprits, so you will just have to play by ear and trust your instincts.

This is not the time to trust anyone too much. Make sure you have covered all your bases though you can never be sure you have done 100% of the job.

You may be the target of politicking in the office but you will triumph eventually if you keep your cool and play smart. Display a Victory Horse near your desk at work or wear one as a pendant/brooch. Stay productive and don't allow yourself to be psychologically unnerved by devils in the workplace.

The three spears here signify three steps of promotion for you.

BUSINESS
TAKE CARE

Beware of getting cheated or conned! Your greed or desire to get rich may land you in hot soup if you fall for scams. While it is possible to make tons of money without having to lift a finger, you are not fated for it this month. Money making opportunities that seem too good to be true probably are.

Don't make big decisions this month as your vision is a wee bit clouded. Maintain the status quo and avoid changes in management or rearrangement of roles. If you have done well for yourself lately, you may be the victim of jealousy, so keep yourself to yourself and don't brag about achievements. Not all are in ecstasy to hear how brilliant you've been lately.

Keep an eagle eye on internal affairs. You can be cheated even by those you consider your own people.

The emblem of the double fish means double abundance. It also means safety for children.

ROMANCE
PRICKLY

Love is not shining this month so don't expect a state of bliss. You are prone to arguments as your love luck is not fantastic. If things continue to bog you down, give yourself time apart as this may be just what you need. Don't get too clingy or you could repel your other half.

You may feel resentful that you have been spending too much on your partner. Don't feel this way as it is infinitely better to squander money on someone you love than lose it on some ill-timed venture! You may suffer a sizeable outflow of funds this month, so might as well direct some to your someone special!

Single Dogs are in for a better time next month, so lay low and hang on tight.

FAMILY
GO HOLIDAY

A great time for family holidays so take off for a vacation with the family. Even if it is a day trip, you will enjoy yourself so much you will feel this is one of the best things you have done lately. Happiness comes in all forms and not just as cash.

Relationship with family is good and harmonious so you will look forward to coming home after work rather than while away evenings at the pub. Share your worries with them as they could give really great advice.

Watch your home security as the Burglary Star can affect the whole household. Make sure all doors and windows are locked and your garden well lit at night.

EDUCATION
AVERAGE

An average time for Dog students. Just another ordinary month with little hope of being Top Dog but at least you won't end up as worst performer either!

School work is OK and manageable. You may find studies tedious and boring as you feel quite listless. While school work does not go badly, you must watch out for your health and sports injuries.

Your active social life and extensive network may interfere with schoolwork. Get your homework done and sorted before you go out to play and party!

The four emblems of scholastic success.

4TH MONTH
MAY 6TH - JUNE 5TH 2008

LUCK FROM HEAVEN

After a lackluster and money-afflicted last month, you are in for a major treat. This month sees money luck flowing in spadefuls into your chart so you can expect some good opportunities to fall into your lap. You even have the luxury to pick and choose which ones appeal to you most! But take care that the juiciest of the lot doesn't pass you by, as there is a chance of you missing out on the biggie!

If you have big dreams, this is the perfect time to pursue them aggressively as the stars are in favour of you realizing your wishes. Even if you have only the foggiest idea of how to go about them, don't worry as somehow you will receive help in achieving your goals. This may be in the form of a mentor as your mentor luck ripens this month and someone will take you under their wing and guide you.

CAREER
SHINING

You have done so well and the accolades pour in so relentlessly you may even feel a bit embarrassed that so much credit is being given to you. As you have earned it, you should bask in the glory since it is not everyday you are so well praised. Though you work as a team and achieve team results, your boss favours you above the rest. Appreciate the kudos graciously but don't get too big for your boots. Don't be too self-deprecating either; if you keep telling others you don't deserve such credit, then they may start to believe you!

Your people skills are thriving and this is an opportune time to expand your network of social and professional contacts. Get involved in societies outside your work. If you can spare the time, apply to be a committee member of professional organizations as they are the best conduits towards meeting like-minded people and others who may prove useful in the future.

A pair of dragons signifies success and courage.

BUSINESS
LUCK IS GOOD

Business luck is good so it is time to dream big, as it is possible your wildest ambitions may stand a chance of coming true. Fortune favours the bold and that applies to you now. A great month to expand, diversify and move on to the next level. Tap your network of friends and associates; they are in a position to help and more important, are willing to do so!

Grapes have flourishing leaves and clusters of fruits, and symbolize an abundant harvest.

Think positive; if you really want to meet someone, just keep nurturing this intention and a situation will arise for you to get up close with your target. Think out of the box; a few pleasant surprises are in store for you. This is the time to be innovative and experiment. Even if you think it won't work, there is no harm in trying unless you have something to lose.

New things that are unfamiliar should not be turned down or written off just because you don't feel like entering forbidden territory. If you can grasp or master some new situations, it could change your life! Wealth luck is very promising, so go for it!

ROMANCE
EXCITING

Plenty of excitement in store when it comes to love. There are heaps of new opportunities to meet interesting new people. Some very fascinating characters may enter your life and spice things up. Single Dogs are in for a great time if you fancy casual liaisons and ships sailing through the night. Lots of light-hearted love for takers!

Married Dogs find their spouses great partners to discuss work and career. They will be an invaluable sounding board for new ideas as their advice will prove useful and help you see things clearer.

Good time to get close to your loved ones. Make time for them as you will be amply pleased with the time and effort invested in them.

The Chinese bulbul and peony is a blessing which means the couple live long together with great honour.

FAMILY
GOOD INFLUENCE

Family and home will prove a big influence on you this month. You may have more domestic responsibilities thrust on you but you are agreeable to be of help wherever possible to your kin. You are also in the mood for some form of home decorating as you feel strongly for home and hearth. This is an auspicious time to invest in improving the home and fixing what needs to be repaired. Even buying a new sofa will put you in a good mood so go for it.

Male Dogs will have a big role to play on the home scene as the household seems to depend on you not only financially but for advice and opinion. Someone in the family is in for a windfall and somehow you are instrumental in making this happen so you feel gratified.

Family wealth augurs well for Dogs and there is plenty of domestic bliss going round. A happy time indeed!

The Wu Lou for health and longevity.

EDUCATION
COMMUNICATIONS

This is the time to communicate with teachers, lecturers and tutors; telling them what you need will help you make the most of your education. Even your parents need to be told about your needs so they understand you better. This is the worst time to suffer in silence! If there is something that worries you, let it be known as people are able to sort it out for you. That's what teachers and parents are for!

Seek out a mentor figure or find someone older and wiser who can take an interest in you. You will be able to progress so much faster. Discuss what is on your mind or what is baffling you of late.

Overall a good month for students. Mixing with kids outside your school or campus will also facilitate your social life.

Apricots indicate good fortune luck for scholars and students.

5TH MONTH
JUNE 6TH - JULY 6TH 2008

MISFORTUNE

Not a happy month as misfortune in one form or another plagues you. The best thing you can do is lie low and take extra care in what you do as even simple things may lead to accidents, damage or loss of money.

There is no money luck and obstacles crop up with irritating regularity to slow progress in whatever you pursue. You can alleviate this with a 5 element pagoda in the Northwest of your home and office.

Anything that involves danger should be avoided; fast driving, excessive drinking, casino gambling, risky sports. You are vulnerable now so if you persist in such activities, you are only making trouble for yourself.

Wear plenty of white, your auspicious colour this month. This will help offset bad luck. Jewellery with auspicious symbols is also particularly powerful in protecting you and promoting your interests.

CAREER
VULNERABLE

You are vulnerable this month so you have to work extra hard just to maintain the status quo. Watch your back all the time. If you have rivals, this may be the time when they can overtake you and you really have to double or triple your effort to keep your head above water. Now is not the time to slack as envious eyes are watching and anything that falls below your usual standards will be noticed and pointed out.

Some mistakes may occur for which you will be blamed. If it was really your fault, best is to come clean and apologize rather than pass the buck. Don't shirk responsibility. You can keep your turf just by being more meticulous and thorough in things you do.

Don't come to work late or you as this will be noted and frowned upon. You have to depend on yourself as others are unable or unwilling to give a helping hand. Your luck is so poor even minor mistakes can be blown out of proportion.

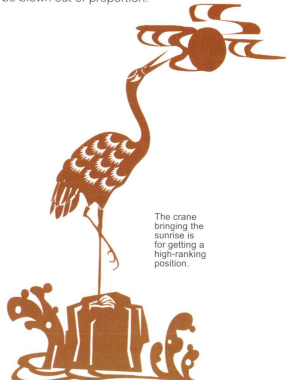

The crane bringing the sunrise is for getting a high-ranking position.

BUSINESS
MODERATE

Be moderate in decision making this month. Don't be too ambitious as the stars are against big dreams, but don't be so scaredy-cat to the extent of being immobile. Postpone important decisions to next month when certain things gel and you can make an informed judgement.

Your best option is to stick to what you have been doing. Maintaining the status quo is the way to go as any heavy investments will not prosper. There is no big money to be made so in order to avoid disappointment, don't nurture any high hopes.

If you have a brilliant idea up your sleeve, keep it there till next month when it can really bear fruit. Anything big you propose or plan now will fall on deaf ears and could be shelved even before it is evaluated. Avoid publicity as any spotlight shining on you now is liable to highlight your faults rather than your talent!

ROMANCE
TENSION

Not a good month for affairs of the heart as there is hidden tension in all your relationships. Big fights can erupt from small misunderstandings and the ball is in your court. Be mature and look at the big picture if you want to settle things quickly. Arguments, if left unchecked, can accumulate so much ill will it can lead to bitter break-ups, so you should take note of the consequences.

If you are serious about your relationship, take the initiative to smooth things out even if you are slightly on the losing end. The *chi* surrounding you now is not conducive for love and you must work extra hard to ensure a happy relationship.

Mandarin ducks always symbolize love

Wear the double happiness symbol for harmony and love in your relationship.

Single Dogs should keep a low profile and not bother searching actively for love. If you are already with someone, wait till next month before making any big move.

FAMILY
HOUSEHOLD SAFETY

Make household safety a priority this month. There is a risk of robbery but the real danger comes from carelessness that can lead to accidents. Make sure everything works and is in good condition. If something needs repairing, like exposed, damaged wires, either fix it or don't use the equipment. Avoid DIY and intensive handiwork around the house. Anything connected to machinery and equipment are prone to being mishandled. If there is repair to be done, get the professionals.

Keep things quiet and low-key as much as possible. Don't throw big, noisy parties as your luck will attract either the wrong people or cause damage to property.

Relationships among family may be strained and there could be one or two big quarrels. Learn to forgive and forget. Even if snide remarks are made against you, just develop a thicker skin. Holding and nursing grudges, real of imagined, can make matters worse, so try be more light-hearted.

EDUCATION
STRESSFUL

Not the best time for education as things may go awry when you least expect. Don't get too easily upset when things go wrong; they are not due to you. This is one of those months when things can't seem to go your way no matter how hard you try, so perhaps you should just sit back, take a deep breath and brace yourself.

Small, silly things can stress you out so don't take matters to heart, especially casual remarks. A betrayal by a friend can put you out of whack; just don't let it affect you too much. Turn the table and make new friends! This could well be the antidote you need.

Sports should be handled with care as you are prone to small injuries. Wear the five element pagoda charm made of gold to protect against negative stars.

6TH MONTH
JULY 7TH - AUGUST 7TH 2008

LOVE & ROMANCE

Loving, romantic time for students, scholars and Dogs in love. With the stars aligned for affairs of the heart, this is the time for everything connected with love, romance and passion.

Dogs are easily inspired as they see more than the sum parts in most things. Many ideas pop into your head and some are extremely productive so let the ideas flow nonstop. Let things suggest themselves to you naturally; don't think or try too hard as this month, things have a way of sorting themselves out to your favour. Only if you consciously try to dam the flow of ideas or work too hard trying to focus will you suffer setbacks and stress.

A generally happy and fulfilling month. With the stars focusing on love, the only thing to beware of is infidelity! You might well be the adulterer or else end as the injured party. Either way, it works against you, so take steps to quell this danger.

CAREER
DARE BE DIFFERENT

Those in the creative industry or in arts, media, entertainment and communications will enjoy an extra advantage this month. You shine and stand out, as suddenly you burst with ideas and most of them are not only workable but profitable!

Dare to be different. It will pay handsome dividends! This is the time to let your creative juices flow unabated. You can suggest even the wildest and most unconventional ideas and they will be considered by powers that be. Certain things and people may not be what they seem but fear not as they are good and will benefit you.

Believe in yourself as there is the risk your modesty will work against you. Others believe and trust you so don't be your own worst enemy! A good time to build rapport with workmates, bosses and outside professionals. The more extensive your network, the better the footing for you. Exploit your contacts and spend time touching base with them; send an email, sms or call them to say hello. A few may even make some profitable offers out of the blue.

Do more than is expected of you if you wish to further your career. This is the time to go somewhere and all you need is some effort.

BUSINESS
GOOD

Great time now to develop friendships and forge ahead with new ones with business associates you hardly know but would wish to build stronger relationships with.

You enjoy good relationship luck so make the most of it. You can make cold calls to people who have never met you and they will be receptive to your proposals. You are easy to get along with and attract all the right people with your vibes. You now have the ability to make small talk, break social barriers and emerge triumphant as even the most snobbish will find time for you.Use this talent to further your career or promote your business. Most deals are forged when a relationship is formed. Invest time and effort to meet customers and to socialize with important suppliers.

You can afford to be revolutionary in your style; perhaps a change in wardrobe or behaviour might improve your image. The way you conduct business can also benefit from a makeover. Rewards come to those who are brave and dare to be different. If you are conservative, the difference is even more dramatic and impressive. Just don't go overboard; make sure you are still in control lest you become a laughing stock!

ROMANCE
FABULOUS

Single Dogs are in for a dramatically thrilling time as you have suitors and admirers thick on the ground. You are particularly attractive to the opposite sex and potential suitors swarm around you as if you are a honey pot. If you are a free person and this is what you fancy, then no harm in being the centre of attention and being courted by several admirers.

Go out, meet new people, party, let your hair down and enjoy life! You have been slaving away and now is the time to sit back and watch the world sashay by. You deserve it. If you are the serious, sensible sort, let go of some responsibilities or else you may end up as a 21st century version of Old Mother Hubbard.

Good time to go steady, propose to your loved one, get married or go on second honeymoon.

Married Dogs must steer clear from situations where they can be tempted into infidelity. It is easy for them to be seduced and tempted since their love luck is strong, but fortunately this also applies to those who already tied the knot. So if you are married, channel all your attention and energies into your better half.

FAMILY
GOOD TIMES

Good times are in store as families who play together stay together and this is very true in your case. Bonding and spending time together doing ordinary things will strengthen ties and reduce chance of infidelity. Quite often in times like these, you get involved in casual flings due to circumstances rather than advanced planning. By staying close to your family, you stay above the fray. And since you are having the time of your life with your nearest and dearest, you will not have stray thoughts either.

Charity work should also be a factor to consider. If things have been going well for you, all the more reason to think of the less fortunate since it is only from a roll of the dice that you are able to enjoy a good life.

Donate time and money and build your store of good karma! You are now personally happier than you have been in some time so now is the best time to spread some joy around. You can also look forward to several happy occasions which are just around the corner.

Pomegranates symbolize prosperity for generation after generation. This means your wealth luck will continue for many generations.

EDUCATION
FAST LEARNER

Time spent revising and going through your studies will pay handsome dividends now as teachers appreciate what you have done. Life is easier since you seem to have an astonishing ability to absorb knowledge like a sponge. Not only do you learn fast, you are able to connect and co-relate various concepts together.

You perform so well some classmates consider you a mini-genius. The studious Dog will go far this month as some form of recognition or award is in the offing. Hard work coupled with that extra spark can transform good work into brilliant results. Your outstanding achievements allow you to tackle things differently and if you are in the creative field, you can be more daring and innovative in your assignments, and able to raise the eyebrows of your lecturers!

Those in creative writing, performing arts, music or fine arts do very well. Ditto for those in science and architecture and law, since they too can be very creative in certain aspects!

New friendships are formed though it may involve a change of alliance as you may have a change of best buddy.

7TH MONTH
AUGUST 8TH - SEPTEMBER 7TH 2008

QUARRELSOME BUT FRUITFUL

A quarrelsome month and most arguments can be attributed to you! You only have yourself to blame if you find yourself being increasingly sidelined. You are more difficult than usual and many find you prickly, sarcastic and overly sensitive. People may find you hard to take, so try to be more laidback. The world is not plotting against you.

Your irritating behaviour may cost you a friend. No one likes a growley dog. You need friends more than ever at this juncture so you are doing yourself a disservice if you continue harping or whining incessantly. Don't make enemies unless there is a reason.

If you feel offended, give the offender the benefit of the doubt. It could have been a misunderstanding. There is also a danger of litigation or lawsuits. If this occurs, settle out of court as you will not fare well in court. Work on your tolerance, keep that temper in check and you should survive nicely this month.

CAREER
BE PROFESSIONAL

Some communication breakdown between you and co-workers which may damage friendships. It's only a notch or two down, so quite easy to patch things up. Be professional about your work as you have a tendency to slack and then hide shoddy work.

If you wish to avoid being criticized then you must deliver the goods. If not, you will be picked upon and if you take it as a personal attack, then things can only worsen and you will make yourself miserable.

You are a no-hoper in meetings and discussions these days due to your temper and insistence on being Mr Right.

Be more pragmatic and don't turn every discussion into a life-or-death debate. Take time to listen to other opinions even if you are convinced your proposal is the best. If you persist in pushing your thoughts and opinions across all the time, you will be excluded from future meetings and be stranded on a desert island.

On the other hand, your popularity is low, so don't trust everyone blindly. Keep your cards close to your chest. Something said in confidence may be used against you so it is better to stay aloof and even appear mysterious if you want to forge ahead.

BUSINESS
PROMISING

You may be feeling on top of the world, invincible and ambitious. This is good but don't make the mistake of stepping on too many toes in your quest to get rich or stay ahead of the competition. You can still be rich and successful and stay popular.

People don't forget easily if you hurt their feelings. If you don't control your passion, you can leave a lasting bad impression which can be detrimental for future alliances.

When attending meetings, restrain yourself and don't give too much away. Be a listener more than speaker. Don't reveal your thoughts too much. You gain more by being a spectator. Don't bother pitching your ideas or selling yourself or going after big contracts. Your luck simply cannot hold. Better lay low than waste a good chance. Postpone important meetings and decisions till next month when your luck improves dramatically.

ROMANCE
LACKING CHARM

Your smooth talking ways which have taken you far appear to fail you this time. Your charm flies out the window and you seem less than appealing. This may bruise your ego somewhat as you may have prided yourself on your charm.

Perhaps you should change your tack this month; don't be too suave as it can be off-putting to some people who find this pretentious. You will score better if you relax and just be yourself. You sometimes try too hard to appear as someone sophisticated or stylish but this does not work all the time and you can end up looking foolish.

This is also not the best time to take your relationship to the next level. You may

Magpies on peach blossom is a sign to usher in auspiciousness and happiness for the loving couple.

encounter some problems like misunderstandings and quarrels. Carry a Wor Ping peace amulet. Display 6 smooth crystal balls in the middle of the living room if you are married. Be nice to your other half to help ensure a hassle free month.

FAMILY
EGOTISTICAL

Your egoistic tendencies may push others away this month. If you have been successful at work of late, don't let it go to your head. Stay grounded and you will enjoy life more.

Relations with siblings may be rocky this month. If you are not in the mood for fraternizing, it is better to avoid them than force the issue with compulsory family meetings. The whole process can be rather unpleasant so it might be best for all parties to avoid each other right now and regroup when the stars are better positioned next month.

Married Dogs may find their in-laws to be a pain as they seem overly keen to meddle in your household. Again, it is better not to invite them over for meals till later.

Five bats surrounding the longevity symbol bring harmony and prosperity.

EDUCATION
SELF MOTIVATION

Self motivation is your best bet this month as you really must concentrate on your work. Don't take too many short cuts or just study certain topics and hope they come out during exams! If you are lazy your grades will suffer badly.

You may feel depressed and distracted if you have a falling out with someone close or who you admire. Don't let that affect you. It is easy for you to feel demoralized these days over minor things as you seem determined to use any excuse to avoid studying!

Share you feelings and worries with your family. They will be of great help and alleviate your doubts. They will also make you feel more secure emotionally and you will be able to concentrate better.

8TH MONTH
SEPTEMBER 8TH - OCTOBER 7TH 2008

ILLNESS & ACCIDENTS

Illness and lack of energy characterize this month for the Dog-born. This seems like a double blow but these two usually accompany each other so you simply must take extra care of your health. Don't ignore your fitness level even if you have always been full of beans. If you sideline the signs, whatever is getting at you can quickly deteriorate into something major. Don't take your health lightly; prevention is much better than cure!

Elderly Dogs are more prone to illness so should be better looked after. Accidents are also another cause for concern so avoid rough sports that can increase chance of injuries. The bright spots? Your career and relationship luck are much better than your health, so you can exploit these even if you are feeling under the weather!

This month is also when you can discover who your real friends are. Someone you never thought of highly may lend an unexpected hand, while the person you thought would stand by you can let you down. Accept help graciously and you should extend such assistance in future too to anyone who needs it.

CAREER
PROMOTION

You may get a big promotion but before you uncork the champagne, you should realize you now have more responsibilities than before. This can increase stress and affect your well being. You will have to work harder to justify the pay raise and elevation of status. Just make sure you don't get burnt out.

Balance your life with enough play time and you can reap the fruits of your harvest. This is not the best time to be daring in whatever you do so better play safe than be sorry. You work better with a partner than alone. It is more advisable to have someone to check and balance as doing it alone can make you prone to carelessness. And you have to take the rap alone too! Search for a suitable work buddy and help each other out.

Make time to get to know colleagues outside work. The contacts you build now will pay off in unexpected ways later so no harm in expanding your network.

Soar high in the sky just like the kite and promotion luck will befall you.

BUSINESS
PROFITABLE

Partnerships work wonderfully for you this month. You have the power to win and let others win too, so this kind of win-win situation is the most compelling reason to go into a new business venture.

The time is ripe for joint ventures and when you join forces with the right party, you will do extremely well. You work well with others and they admire your talent and people skills.

If you can find someone intelligent, you will enjoy life even more as the intellectual simulation will be the impetus and inspire you to new heights. You need this someone to suggest the money-making idea and you can take over from there.

With new incentives and profits rolling in, you begin to enjoy working hard again! Avoid people who criticize you unfairly or make you feel down. You don't need to feel bad about yourself as you know your skills and limits, so you can do very well without these rainers on your parade.

Place the Ru Yi, a symbol of authority, on the left side of your desk or behind you to attract respect from colleagues.

ROMANCE
BLOOMING

Single Dogs in search of life partners can find the person of their dreams this month. Even if it doesn't end in marriage, this person can continue to be a major influence in your life. If you are hot on tying the nuptial knot, display your Peach Blossom animal and see what happens!

Don't shy away from blind dates as who knows what that might lead to? You can fall for someone very unexpected, someone that even you had always assumed would be improbable; so never say never! Stay open to new ideas and you are on your way to good times!

If you are already attached, life gets even better! You are in the mood for love, passion and drama this month and can really let yourself go with your spouse. Things could heat up like when you first met!

"Kam Yoke Mun Thong" means your house is filled with gold and jade. This indicates wealth luck is filling your home with prosperity.

FAMILY
ILLNESS *CHI*

The Illness Star hovers restlessly above you and can affect your whole family if left unchecked. If you are down with flu, stay home to rest and recover. This is better than battling it by continuing to go to work, as you can fall seriously ill later or spread your bug to all your colleagues.

Wear a Wu Lou pendant or carry one with you. The illness energies are strong as it has been enhanced this month by a monthly star.

The younger and older generations get on famously so at least you can look forward to sharing some of the joy. Communicate more with the older generation and you will enjoy the benefits as you begin to see what makes the other generation tick!

EDUCATION
SLOW PACE

A sad lack of energy can get you down in more ways than one, so an extra dose of vitamins and citrus juices won't be amiss. You are easily tired so don't push yourself too hard, more so if there doesn't seem to be a root cause.

However, rest assured your lecturers won't accept shoddy work regardless of your stamina levels so you must allow yourself good time to finish all assignments. Start early and take your time as your pace may have slowed noticeably. This way, you can keep your head bobbing above water. Begin as soon as you are given the topics; this will save you plenty of stress as the deadline nears.

You may be asked to mediate and play the part of diplomat in the case of two friends fighting. Your quarrelsome nature from last month has vanished and been replaced by your good natured self, so now you can relish the new role as peacemaker since you would be in the position to know!

The Chi Lin brings you all the emblems of scholastic success.

9TH MONTH
OCTOBER 8TH - NOVEMBER 6TH 2008

NEW BEGINNINGS

This is a great month that sees many positive changes. An important, transformational period that brings dramatic shifts in your life. Don't be averse to changing directions halfway as fortune favours new beginnings at this time of the year.

Changing your goals is neither a sin nor a crime. It doesn't make you a better or worse person. Factors may have changed to force a rethink, so this does not mean you have failed in attaining your previous goals. If you want change, don't stick stubbornly to what you expected before. Go with the flow and see where the tide takes you. Your new destination may be a revelation.

Some big changes may affect your status quo; this could be a job change, work promotion, moving house or even moving to a new town/country. The changes are mostly for good though some may seem like the opposite at first. Your overall luck is well positioned and whatever changes bounce into your life are usually accompanied by positive results.

CAREER
INFLUENTIAL

You have some newfound influence this month and others seem willing to buckle under your supervision, even those who had been reluctant to co-operate earlier. If you can use this skill successfully in your job, you will do very well!

There may be some major changes or linear shifts in the workplace; you may be promoted, or transferred to a nice new project or new department altogether. Even if you feel alien, you should be able to adapt fast to your new environment. Just think positive and set your mind to the inevitable.

Maintain old colleagues as friends even if you moved up or away to a different building. Someone new may join your section or team. You should get on well with this person.

You are about to enter another great period of your life with far-reaching effect. Be prepared for exciting things coming your way in the next few months as interesting things are set to happen in your career.

The victory horse that flies even faster than the magpie is a symbol of winning over the competition.

Sailing ship
brings wealth
from the winds
and waters.

BUSINESS
BUSINESS LUCK

Business luck is booming and is reaching its zenith so you can expand and invest safely this month. If you are planning a new subsidiary or a new business altogether, this is the best time. Go ahead with confidence.

There may be some dispute if you are in partnership with someone in business. For now, it is better to work and slave away on your own rather than work with too many people as everyone seems determined to run the show for you.

Go with your instincts on big decisions as what you finally decide should turn out well. Don't let others unduly influence you as you are supposed to be the one wielding the big stick!

Dog bosses involved in media, sales, finance, communications and public relations will do particularly well.

ROMANCE
INDULGENT

Time to enjoy, pamper yourself and indulge in some decadent ways!

Let your heart rule rather than your head. You are filled with passion, love and desire. Once you leave the office, you should also leave all work worries behind. If not, you will simply be lugging excess baggage that does you no good, since nothing can be done till you are back at your work desk.

Take time out to enjoy your personal life. Single Dogs have no problem finding their mates since your charm level is relatively high. Many are enchanted by your looks, social niceties and style, so the more parties you attend, the more connections you enjoy. Meeting and mingling do wonders for your ego so you should not think too deeply but just relax and take advantage of the situation.

Learn to let your hair down; don't be too picky or judgemental since you don't have to marry the first person you meet! Anyway, first impressions don't count much right now.

A phoenix flying around a peony blossom implies a continuous stream of good things and a happy life.

FAMILY
HOME MAKEOVER

Now is an opportune time for a big makeover on the home front. Even if you are not into décor, you may find yourself buying some home improvement and interior design magazines for inspiration!

Elephant carryng an evergreen plant implies that you will have good fortune and riches forever.

Even doing something as minor as buying a side table, lamp or decorative knick-knack can give you much pleasure. Do some spring cleaning and clear out the clutter. Old things have not seen or used in a long while and long forgotten should be discarded or given away. A spot of repainting or repairing will do wonders to the overall look of the house. And increase its value!

Dogs with young children will find their parental roles expanded but this is something you will relish so all's well, even if you collapse in a heap at the end of the day. Your kids will give you a fantastic time and bring much joy and contentment.

EDUCATION
HAPPY

This is a happy period for campus Dogs. You feel perky most of the time which also affects those near to you as your natural joy of life is infectious. Everything falls into place and you do well as you are feeling great about life. There is so much going for you at this moment. Indeed you wish there were more hours in the day for you to enjoy.

You realize learning and studying need not be a chore and can and should be a pleasure. Once you confirm this mindset, your life gets even better as you begin to treat education as a vocation, something to sink your teeth into.

Your school and social life are so hectic you may end up burning your candle at both end. Make sure you get enough sleep or you could end up unlikeably cranky.

The magnolia, iris and orchid denote talent.

10TH MONTH
NOVEMBER 7TH - DECEMBER 6TH 2008

HIGH ENERGY

The good spell you enjoyed last month continues unabated this month so you have more reasons to toast the good life. Since the prevailing factor is energy, you are bursting with strength and power. However you are only human despite what you think, so avoid taking on too many responsibilities as you may be unable to cope.

Don't let personal pride get in the way. You may be convinced you can be like Superman, but if you falter, there is nothing embarrassing about making a U-turn. Better admit you have bitten off more than you can chew than mess things up to the point where serious damage occurs and you have to pay.

You need to rope in friends and allies as some important projects need their input however qualified you may be. Since your energy is at boiling point, you can make extra cash easily, but these will be small amounts so don't bank on these extra revenues to buy that dream penthouse.

CAREER
BUSY TIME

Busy, hectic period but luckily you are popular with your peers now so all is well. Your colleagues and superiors take a shine to you and recognize the hard work you put in. You get saddled with more responsibilities but you seem to be coping very well. If the deadlines are unreasonable, you should insist on an extension rather than submitting shoddy work.

Those in high stress occupations must give themselves time out to rest, relax and recover. Your climb up the corporate ladder seems unencumbered with petty obstacles and this may give you a false impression that you are infallible. Don't let this get to your head and do not trample on others just to show off you can. You will get away now but people you hurt for amusement will not forget or forgive easily.

The more allies you have, the more you can achieve. So make friends everywhere rather than cultivate jealousy.

When a Crimson Phoenix brings you a silk ribbon, it means the luck of fame and glory is coming to you. You will soon receive recognition for your efforts.

BUSINESS
NETWORK

Busy and profitable time for those in the communications business like printing, publishing and performing arts. Those in PR are well positioned to maximize profits.

This symbol of lotus leaves having deep roots and luxuriant leaves symbolizes a solid foundation and vigorous development in business.

You are particularly sweet-mouthed this period and can close deals quickly. However, your luck dictates no huge gains, so don't expect torrents of cash. Wealth Luck arrives in full force only next month, so now is the time to consolidate and build on foundations. Take calculated risks and only in areas where you have expertise. Charting unknown territories is a no-go at this time.

You seem besieged with ideas and most are not really worthwhile, so try to slow your mind down as it seems to be working overtime on irrelevant and unprofitable ideas. Don't let disconnected thoughts dominate; make an effort to steady your train of thought.

ROMANCE
LUCKY IN LOVE

A romantic and lust-filled month for Dogs keen on the idea. If you have love on your mind, you will attract others who share the same inclinations so you should be seeing some fireworks behind closed doors.

Single Dogs who are footloose and fancy-free are particularly exposed to romantic encounters and one night stands if this is what you want. You meet people who fascinate you due mostly to their unrelated field of work to yours. You can even find your soulmate or someone special you wish to spend the rest of your life with.

Going steady, getting engaged or getting married are on the cards as this is an auspicious period for affairs concerning the heart.

Married Dogs who have already found their life partners should avoid any temptations of the flesh; it will come to no good. Wear the double happiness symbol to avoid risky rendezvous!

The double happiness sign is incredibly lucky as a symbol of romance.

FAMILY
BUSY

Your home and hearth are filled with laughter and activity so this is a very pleasant time. You enjoy returning home but sometimes wish your partner can help out more, as you feel like the only doing all the work while he/she glides past merrily with the kids.

Talk to your spouse and family if you feel you are being used or taken for granted. Delegate some chores to others and stand firm that you have more than enough to do. Don't suffer or harbour vengeful thoughts in silence. You may be surprised how understanding they can be. Building bridges between the kids and your siblings take on extra urgency this month. You feel it is time to reconnect and you will be well pleased you did so.

The symbol of longevity with five bats.

EDUCATION
GREAT

You have an excellent time in store this month; everything goes well and you may even receive an award of some sort. Perhaps even a scholarship if you are the academic type!

For once you actually look forward to exams, knowing full well you will do well! Not only are your grades looking good, so are you! Your sparkling personality will get you far. Teachers warm to you and pals think you are Top Dog and most likely they are correct too!

Good time now to set higher standards for yourself as only you know how far you can rise. At the end of the day, even you will be surprised at your own talents.

11TH MONTH
DECEMBER 7TH 2008 - JANUARY 5TH 2009

WEALTH & PROSPERITY

This month heralds fabulous opportunities to not only make money but to enjoy the fruits of your labour. As you take stock of the last ten months and look forward to the next two before the new lunar year takes over, you can truly reflect on the many achievements and give yourself a pat on the back.

Wealth luck is flowing in nonstop and accompanied by fame and recognition luck as well, so this promises to be one of the best times of the year for the Dog.

If you have been unsure of some important things, now is the best time to firm up your final decisions. You have seldom been more confident than now, and with the stars lining up in your favour, few things can go wrong. This is also a spiritual time for you as you rake in material wealth. If you donate some to charity, you will enhance your karma tremendously at this juncture of your life.

CAREER
CAREER LUCK

Career luck peaks this month and if you are angling for a promotion or new job, you will get what your heart desires. Work has never been easier or more fun. Your productivity reaches new heights and you seem to be a one-man show bringing in the profits and new contracts.

Your boss stops short of offering you a partnership but makes up for it with plenty of perks like an expense account on company car. You may enter management level or be in line to be a director. Demonstrate some leadership if you want to be seen as one. Even if this feels alien to you, others will still think you have what it takes.

You may require some outside contact to power ahead, so exploit your data base. You are in such demand others you hardly know are eager to be your friend as your reputation has preceded you.

BUSINESS
FANTASTIC

You are being swamped with money-making opportunities and business is booming. Perhaps it is due to the traditional year end jump in sales augmented by recent innovations introduced recently which are now bearing fruit.

Golden ingots bring luck and prosperity.

A very busy period signaling a prosperous balance sheet filled with black ink. Since you are flushed with cash, this allows another window to open as you can invest in new subsidiary, joint venture or takeover. Or simply increase your stake in your favourite counters in the share market. Your Midas touch becomes obvious when certain stocks you pick jump in value quickly!

Projects that had been languishing take on new momentum and can be wrapped up successfully, providing yet another channel for more funds to flow in. All these and an unexpected windfall make December a major contributor to your annual balance sheets!

ROMANCE
RATIONAL

Instead of rushing headlong into lovemaking as you are wont to do, this period sees a more introspective single Dog. Your head dominates instead of your heart. You become more analytical, objective and even aloof. This does not go down well with your partner which can lead to arguments over your perceived coldness.

Your passion is at odds with what is happening in your life. Though your finances are rosier than expected, you seem more reluctant than ever to show your emotions. You think this is for the better since you are more concerned about the long term, but to ensure there is one, you should also demonstrate some passion! Otherwise your future might end with you being by your solitary self.

Married Dogs also do not fare so well as you need a serious talk to sort out who should be in charge of what. You seem picky and demanding and if you think being the dominant partner is your cup of tea, let the other person know. Note that role-playing has its limits.

FAMILY
FULFILLING

The evergreen pine tree is often associated with longevity.

A lot of your pent-up energies seem to be directed towards your family or if unmarried, towards your parents and siblings. You are in the mood to develop relationships or repair damaged ones. You derive much satisfaction from being around your clan and kids. You feel particularly close to blood relations and are more than happy to buy them presents and take them out for treats like expensive dinners.

Since you are now loaded with cash, you can afford to take them for a great holiday. Anything or anywhere you choose will have the same effect; a happy time.

Home decorations and improvement are the order of the day as it is very auspicious to renovate your home. Start redecorating the Northwest which is your lucky corner this month. Patriarchs will find they have increased authority.

EDUCATION
AUSPICIOUS

You are loaded with luck this time and what you put your mind will quickly bear fruit. Studying comes easy and good grades are for the taking. If you had been less than a stellar performer lately, now this is your turn to shine again.

Your learning rate shoots up and even if you were not much of a scholar, you seem attracted now to the thought of a post graduate degree. If you are an 'A' student, the sky's the limit!

Making your mark in the classroom and lecture hall means getting noticed and admired by both teachers and fellow students. Impressions made now will be long-lasting, so put in your best effort.

This symbol is for excellence in scholastic talents.

12TH MONTH
JANUARY 6TH - FEBRUARY 3RD 2009

DANGER OF ROBBERY

A sober month to end the lunar year before a new one begins. You have enjoyed so much luck and easy money even you were beginning to wonder how long your winning streak can last. Perhaps now is the hour of reckoning.

New and unexpected expenses crop up, eating into your profits. While it is not too bad to have reduced income, there is also the chance of losing money earned previously. If you lose small amounts, be thankful and do not bother to try retrieving it as you would be throwing good money away chasing after the bad.

Some money luck remains with you so there is still hope you can recoup but from other sources, not the ones which lost you money. But your winning streak seems to have ended as revenues are small compared to last month's massive infusion.

CAREER
RIVALS

If you have enemies or rivals in the ranks, they can work against you since your luck is down. The problem is that these people do not show their hands openly so you are not on a level playing field. It is tough to know who is on your side and who is plotting your downfall! Not a good time to trust others so you should hold your cards close to your chest.

Display a rooster on your desk if things get out of hand since you may be victim of a malicious gossip or office politics. Don't take it lying down because if you fight back, you will win. All you need is a clear head and you are able to turn the table on anyone in the way.

Be seen as a dependable workhorse and soon others will begin to speak well of you.

BUSINESS
STATUS QUO

The best advice is to maintain your existing status quo! Even if you lose money or sales drop, this is seen as unavoidable; just as you made so much easy money recently, it stands to reason you can lose it too if you are not careful.

You are at risk of being conned or cheated by some suave, smooth talker who tries to convince you to invest in dubious schemes. If you are getting used to easy money, this may prove to be your wake-up call!

This symbol of egret, reed and lotus symbolizes smooth business development.

Maintain your current management style and leave any reshuffle till next month. Keep low and avoid publicity. Postpone all signing ceremonies, press conferences or launching of new products. If unavoidable, let someone else take the limelight. You can play the role of benign observer. Any attention drawn to you is either ineffective or will highlight your faults. Keep your eye on your private accounts as this is another risk prone area.

ROMANCE
NOT STEAMING

Love luck is not in full bloom and hence your love life is not peaches and cream either. You are more argumentative and will not take 'yes' or 'no' (depending on the situation!) for an answer. Maybe a brief respite from each other is best for both parties. On the other hand, don't get too clingey.

Single Dogs are not going anywhere either. No point searching for true love as your luck is out of sync. If desperate, go clubbing with friends. Don't expect much and you may meet someone nice. The more you expect, the less chance it will happen.

FAMILY
VACATION

Good time to take off with the family. Doing so will ease tensions between you and spouse as new sights and sounds will push all minor worries and irritations to the back burner. You enjoy a harmonious relationship with the family. Include the kids in family discussions. Something they say in innocence may be of aid and help you see things clearer.

Anything that is not urgent can wait till your return. Your luck dictates the further you go away from your base, the better. You will return refreshed and full of beans. Perhaps you may even meet some supplier or business contact.

But your home may be afflicted by the Burglary Star; nothing serious but if you have an alarm system, make sure it works and all doors/windows are locked. Inform your neighbours.

Tortoises are an emblem of longevity.

EDUCATION
AVERAGE

Dogs getting an education will fare averagely; nothing sensational to look forward to but nothing detrimental either. So if you find lessons a yawn, be grateful you are not being asked to make any presentation for which you are so ill prepared!

Your health is more cause for worry; you seem to fall for every flu bug going around so watch out, as the slightest fever may end up in bed when you would rather be clubbing. Active, physical sports should be avoided as bruises, cuts and more may upset your studies and social life. Cut down on gymming. Since you are lack luster in studies, so make sure all homework and assignments are completed before you jet off to the mall.

Part Three

- **DOG'S PERSONALIZED FENG SHUI IN 2008**

- **FENG SHUI CHART OF 2008**

- **PRODUCTS TO ENHANCE LUCK IN 2008**

THE DOG'S PERSONALIZED FENG SHUI IN 2008

Type of Dog (HS/EB)	Western Calendar Dates	Age	Kua Number Males	Kua Number Females
Wood Dog	14 Feb 1934 to 3 Feb 1935	74	3 East Group	3 East Group
Fire Dog	2 Feb 1946 to 21 Jan 1947	62	9 East Group	6 West Group
Earth Dog	18 Feb 1958 to 7 Feb 1959	50	6 West Group	9 East Group
Metal Dog	6 Feb 1970 to 26 Jan 1971	38	3 East Group	3 East Group
Water Dog	25 Jan 1982 to 12 Feb 1983	26	9 East Group	6 West Group
Wood Dog	10 Feb 1994 to 30 Jan 1995	14	6 West Group	9 East Group
Fire Dog	29 Jan 2006 to 17 Feb 2007	2	3 East Group	3 East Group

USE THE FOLLOWING WAYS TO IMPROVE YOUR FENG SHUI IN 2008

1. Protecting and Enhance the Dog direction
2. West Group Dogs Activate your Northeast direction
3. East Group Dogs Activate your East direction
4. Create Affinity Triangle of *Tien Ti Ren* – light up South 2, NW1 & NE3 with sun & moon sign

PROTECTING & ENHANCING YOUR DOG DIRECTION

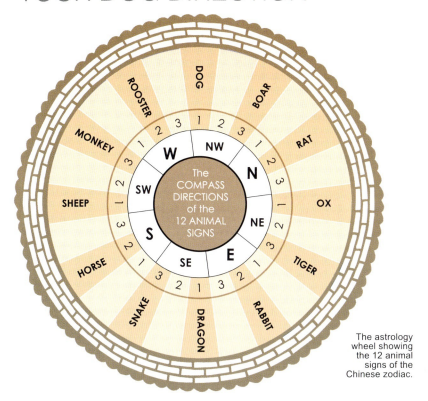

The astrology wheel showing the 12 animal signs of the Chinese zodiac.

The Dog's direction is NW1 and this is shown in the compass wheel above, which demarcates the 8 main directions into 24 direction categories of fifteen degrees each. In feng shui, these directions are known as the 24 mountains of the compass. In Chinese astrology we use every alternate one of the 24 mountains (or directions) to assign to each of the twelve animal signs. The four animal signs of the zodiac that occupy the cardinal directions are the Rat in the North; the Rabbit in the East; the Horse in the South and the Rooster in the West. Each of these animal signs occupies the central subdirections of North 2, East 2, South 2 and West 2 respectively.

The other animal signs have their locations in the secondary directions; thus we have the Ox and the Tiger in NE1 and NE3 respectively; the Dragon and the Snake in SE1 and SE3; the Sheep and the Monkey in SW1 and SW3; and the Dog and the Boar in NW1 and NW3.

Those born in the year of the Dog must protect and enhance their home direction of Northwest 1. Look for this sector in their home or office making sure the Northwest sector of your house is not afflicted in any way by any harmful or hostile physical structures either in the outside environment or in the interiors. Harmful physical structures shoot secret poison arrows that create bad feng shui to residents of the household. Poison arrows send killing *chi*, which must be deflected or remedied. When the Northwest sector of your house is afflicted, it has the potential to hurt residents born in the year of the Dog.

HARMFUL PHYSICAL STRUCTURES OF THE ENVIRONMENT

The outside environment that surrounds your home can often have physical structures that send bad energy towards your home bringing lethal bad effects without you even knowing it hence these are called secret poison arrows. Some of these structures include a straight road coming directly towards the front door resembling an arrow or a bullet bringing killing energy, the edge of a tall or large building bringing destructive cutting energy; a big building that is too close to your front door which blocks the good *chi* from entering your home; a transmission tower that creates blockages to your good luck and also sends harmful energy your way; an elevated road which slices into the energy field of your home, or any physical structure that appears threatening or hostile. Large structures that overwhelm your home almost always blocks your luck and if anything sharp, angular or pointed and straight are directly aimed at your front door, these are certain to bring serious feng shui afflictions.

The harmful effects of fearsome structures in the environment are often the cause of bad feng shui. This kind of harmful *chi* brings misfortune luck that is usually hard to overcome and that

may require the attention of a feng shui expert. Having said that it is easy enough to initiate some simple measures to protect and enhance the sector that is most important to you according to your animal sign.

Firstly, those born in the year of the Dog must ensure that the Northwest sector of the house is not directly hit by any harmful outside structure irrespective of whether or not the main door is located there. However, if there IS a door here, whether it is a main or secondary sliding door, then it is even more necessary to place a cure or remedy to overcome the negative impact of the physical structure.

If the structure is coming towards the Northwest, we assume the bad energy is coming from the opposite direction i.e. from the Southeast (this means the house is sitting NW). If this is the case then creating some kind of "metal" presence between the house and the physical structure is the remedy. Metal here can be a windchime or a bell. The metal energy will defeat afflicted wood energy coming towards the house from the Southeast.

If the house is facing Northwest on the other hand, then the afflicted energy is coming from a metal direction. In this case the remedy will be bright lights to overcome the afflicted metal energy.

If you live in an apartment and there is an offending structure within view of your window or balcony, and the direction it is coming from is the Southeast, it is necessary to place a metal windchime or metal bell between the structure and the window of your apartment. The metal sounds made by the windchime will subdue the afflicted energy coming towards the SE facing window or balcony of your apartment. The idea is to create this metal element remedy between the offending structure and the apartment sector that is afflicted.

Secondly, the Dog direction should also not be hurt by any negative intangible energy caused by the flight of numbers in the annual flying star chart. This changes from year to year.

In 2008, the Northwest is afflicted by the presence of the illness star 2, which tends to bring problems related to health and fitness concerns. So in 2008 the Dog direction is not auspicious as its annual flying star hurts it. The location of NW1 requires the presence of a suitable metal element cure. A brass metal Wu Lou will help to subdue the illness *chi* here quite effectively.

In placing the cure here do get your metal windchimes form a shop with good healthy energy. The worst is to buy feng shui remedies that are sold in dirty places as the energy picked up tends to be sickly and unlucky.

> **NOTE** Use the compass to determine the Dog direction inside your home. It is advisable to use a floor plan to identify the sector of the house, and that of individual rooms that correspond to the Dog direction more easily. It is as important checking the Dog sector of the whole house (known as the big *tai chi* of your house) as it is to check the Dog sector of your bedroom or study or any room where you spend most of your time.

Thirdly it is beneficial feng shui for Dog people to ensure that the toilet, storeroom or kitchen is not located in the NW1 sector of their home, house or apartment, as this can cause misfortune to befall the Dog person living in the house.

A toilet in the Dog direction flushes away the vital essence of the Dog person's luck causing something negative to occur in his/her career luck. Success is hard to come by and deals are hard to close. Those in business are especially affected as luck will get unceremoniously flushed away!

A storeroom in the Dog direction cause the Dog's good luck potential to be "locked up" making it hard to attain ambitions. It is like having your life clogged up with junk. If you have this feature in your home, convert the storeroom into a usable area. Install a bright light and apply a new coat of paint and you will see your life improve!

A kitchen in the Dog direction compromises any good fortune that the Dog enjoys as it is pressed down by the fire energy of the kitchen. Do make an effort to relocate the kitchen; especially if it is the patriarch who is the Dog born.

NOTE When the toilet, storeroom or kitchen occupies the Dog location in your house, and you cannot do anything about it, at least ensure there are no Dog images/paintings placed there. Never activate afflicted space. The best remedy for an afflicted Dog corner in 2008 is to have fire or water element energy present.

ENHANCING THE DOG DIRECTION IN 2008

For the coming year, the Dog direction benefits from having the energy of the star of Small Luck i.e. luck in all the little things that make up the sum total of life and living. The star of Small Luck is to be welcomed as it ensures that daily aggravations will disappear and your life becomes a great deal more settled and harmonious.

It is beneficial to place some kind of auspicious urn, vase or other container and fill with semi precious stones as this will serve to expand your luck. What is interesting is that your ally the Tiger also enjoys the star of Small Luck and this makes them effective as allies in 2008. A partnership between a Tiger and Dog will enjoy Small Luck.

In 2008, the flying star number of the Northwest direction is 2 which is an earth number, so it is important that this afflictive star does not inadvertently get strengthened by the presence of too many lights in this sector. Instead there should be more metal energy to strengthen the sector and press down on the illness star.

Also note that in the year 2008 there is a serious shortage of metal element and this is needed to balance out the elements of the year. Bringing gold to the Dog direction is a powerful enhancing agent in 2008 for Dog born people.

You can also display a replica of the beautiful liu li urn filled with plenty of jewels and place it in the Dog direction. This adds substance and quantity to the star of Small Luck, which is in your direction this year.

Beautiful liu li urn filled with plenty of jewels.

FEMALE DOG & THE EIGHT MANSIONS FORMULA

AUSPICIOUS DIRECTIONS FOR DOG WOMEN

The four lucky directions for Dog women are shown in the table below. They too have Kua numbers 3, 6 or 9 and they too belong to both the East and West group. Women born in 1946 and 1982 belong to the West group and their Kua number is 6. Like the men, women who belong to the West group find that three of their four auspicious directions are afflicted – i.e. West, NW and

Year of Birth	1934	1946	1958	1970	1982	1994	2006
HS element of the year/Kua#	Wood 3	Fire 6	Earth 9	Metal 3	Water 6	Wood 9	Fire 3
Success Direction	South	West	East	South	West	East	South
Health Direction	North	NE	SE	North	NE	SE	North
Love & Family Direction	SE	SW	North	SE	SW	North	SE
Personal Growth Direction	East	NW	South	East	NW	South	East
Age in 2008	74	62	50	38	26	14	2

SW. The West direction, which is their *sheng chi* direction, is hurt by the number 3 hostility star, which brings quarrels and misunderstandings. The number 2 illness star afflicts the Northwest direction while the Southwest direction has the robbery and burglary star 7.

West group Dog women find that only the Northeast sector is the only direction for them to face. As this is the home direction of the Tiger (an ally of the Dog), the NE direction has added positive potency. They should thus activate this sector of their living room or office.

Dog born women who belong to the East group have Kua numbers 3 or 9. Those having 9 as their *sheng chi* will find 2008 to be especially lucky for them in terms of their work and career luck and this is because

their *sheng chi* direction of East enjoys excellent luck this year. Those whose Kua number is 3 however will find that 2008 is not as lucky for them. This is because their *sheng chi* direction of South is extremely afflicted and in fact all through the year they should make very certain they do not face the South direction. Instead they should face East to capture the luck of 8.

All East group people should in fact not face South or North, and then the year will be smooth for them. They should not face North in 2008 even if North is auspicious for them. This is because North is where *Tai Sui* resides and facing North incurs his wrath.

Facing South is even worse as South is where the dreadful Five Yellow resides, Even if this is one of your lucky directions you are strongly advised not to face South all through 2008 when doing any important work and definitely do not to sleep with your head pointed to the South direction. It is also a major taboo in 2008 to activate the South with lights. This will only make the affliction stronger attracting misfortune.

It is an excellent idea for East group Dog women to activate the East direction, which is highly auspicious in 2008. Place plenty of plants here and definitely have a water feature in the East to strengthen the *chi* of the direction. The star of reducing energy hurts the East but with water this is easily corrected.

MALE DOGS & THE EIGHT MANSIONS FORMULA

The table on the facing page shows the four auspicious directions for Dog men born in Dog years starting from 1934. These directions are calculated according to the Eight Mansions formula of feng shui. Note that everyone born in Dog years have Kua numbers 3, 6 or 9 and this set of parent string numbers indicate that Dog people enjoy their best luck during the cycles of periods 3,6 and 9. So it will

be the Period of 9 when they all benefit the most.

Eight Mansions feng shui divides people into East and West groups, with each group having their own lucky and unlucky directions. There are different ways to apply the Eight Mansions formula either on its own or in conjunction with other feng shui methods and formulas. An easy way to

AUSPICIOUS DIRECTIONS FOR DOG MEN

Year of Birth	1934	1946	1958	1970	1982	1994	2006
HS element of the year/Kua#	Wood 3	Fire 9	Earth 6	Metal 3	Water 9	Wood 6	Fire 3
Success Direction	South	East	West	South	East	West	South
Health Direction	North	SE	NE	North	SE	NE	North
Love & Family Direction	SE	North	SW	SE	North	SW	SE
Personal Growth Direction	East	South	NW	East	South	NW	East
Age in 2008	74	62	50	38	26	14	2

benefit from Eight Mansions is to determine your auspicious directions and make sure that no matter what you are doing – be it sitting at your desk and working, giving a lecture or presentation, sleeping, eating dating or negotiating, if you make the effort to always face at least one of your good directions you are certain to enjoy good feng shui all the time.

In 2008 West group Dog men have a hard time choosing a suitable facing direction as three out of four of their auspicious directions is afflicted.

For success luck, always sit facing your *sheng chi* direction unless it is afflicted this year. The *sheng chi* direction brings maximum growth and is an excellent direction to face at work. Arrange your desk so you sit facing your personal *sheng chi*. But watch that you are not being hit by poison arrows like overhead beams, edge of corners or long corridors coming straight at you.

If you observe these tips, you are sure to enjoy excellent feng shui. If you have to choose between tapping a direction and being hit by a poison arrow, it is better not to get hit by the poison arrow.

They will meet with quarrelsome vibes if they sit facing West in 2008. In fact, during the year 2008, anyone belonging to the West group have a tough choice facing them and this is because three of their four auspicious directions are afflicted – i.e. West, NW and SW. The West direction, which is their health or romance direction, is hurt by the number 3 hostility star, which brings quarrels and misunderstandings.

The Dog's own Northwest direction is afflicted by the number 2 illness star, while the Southwest direction has the robbery and burglary star 7. The West direction suffers from the hostility star which brings aggravating quarrelsome energy.

West group Dog men will find it hard to actualize success luck in 2008 and may have flawed relationship luck and little chance of growing as a person. Attempts at self-development will be flawed and bound to encounter obstacles.

For the West group Dog men therefore their Kua number of 6 brings few choices. Only the Northeast sector of the house or office is blessed with a positive star, so this direction is the best one for them to face. As this is the home direction of the Tiger (an ally of the Dog), the NE sector takes on added potency for Dog people. So if you are a West group Dog guy, you can activate this sector of your living room or office.

All Dog men and especially those with a West group Kua number will benefit from living in a house that enjoys the SW/NE orientation especially one facing SW1. These are very special houses, as those of you who are acquainted with Flying Star feng shui will know. All recently built SW and NE facing houses will bring extreme good fortune to the West group Dog born male irrespective of their heavenly stem elements. This house brings plenty of wealth luck in the Period of 8 as well as excellent relationship and health luck. There is protection against premature death and illnesses is kept at bay.

NOTE Carry a good pocket compass to ensure you are never at a loss when it comes to checking directions prior to sitting down to work. This is an easy way of practising basic feng shui.

Always use a compass to take directions if you want to get your feng shui right.

CREATE AFFINITY TRIANGLE OF *TIEN TI REN*

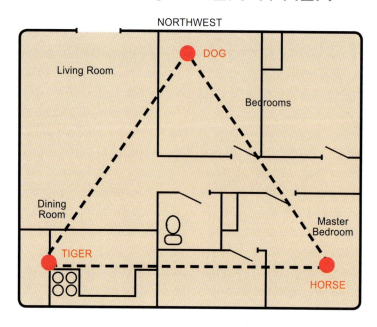

Create affinity triangle of *Tien Ti Ren* – light up NW1, South 2 & NE3; with sun & moon sign. One of the most powerful aspects of astrological feng shui is the concept of "borrowing luck". In updating one's feng shui from year to year, it is always necessary to investigate the energy affecting the 12 animal signs in each New Year. This is because the quality of each sign's energy changes.

Knowing the affinity triangles of the zodiac is also important.

There are altogether four triangles of affinity. For the Dog, the other two animal signs that make up its triangle of affinity are the Horse and the Tiger. These three animals are described as being allies and each can "borrow" the good luck of the other two and it is in fact lucky to do so.

It is really marvelous for all three animal signs when all three signs that make up any affinity triangle enjoy equal good fortune in any year, although this is rarely the case.

Whether the good luck comes from the flying star annual chart or from the luck stars of the twenty four mountains, it is necessary to check the luck of one's astrological allies. In 2008, the Dog's ally the Tiger enjoys good fortune as the romance and studying star

4 is complemented by the auspicious star of Small Luck.

The other ally, the Horse, unfortunately does not have a good year, being terribly afflicted in 2008. We know that the Dog's luck is mixed with a propensity to illness. However, the Dog also enjoys the Star of Small Luck.

On balance, we note that the triangle of affinity made up of the Dog and its allies is not particularly strong as the Horse is so afflicted, thereby creating a weak link here. Nevertheless, lighting up an affinity triangle to signify heaven, earth and mankind - *Tien Ti Ren* - is most auspicious. This is a very powerful feng shui feature and although not all the three locations of the Dog, Horse and Tiger affinity are equally lucky, nevertheless, in unity there is certain to be good fortune.

Dog people should thus ensure that they enjoy the special magic of *Tien Ti Ren* by lighting up the three directions that corresponds to the three animal signs i.e. the NW1, the NE3, and the South 2 direction. Place three bright lights in these three corners of the house.

Keep these three friendly corners lit up with bright lights. Glitter lamps with moving bits, which come in different colours, are very effective for creating this feng shui feature. Please make very sure that you are accurate in your compass reading when building your triangle of affinity. Keep the lights turned on for at least three hours each night. You may also use the wealth tree of lights and coins placed in three corners to create a powerful *Tien Ti Ren* triangle.

You can also place the sun and moon sign – a circle floating above a crescent – in each corner in front of the light. This completes the affinity triangle, which brings auspicious good fortune to everyone residing in the home irrespective of their animal sign. The sun and moon sign brings the luck of wealth creation.

Glitter lamps make good activators for lucky sectors.

One more thing you can do. If the secret friend of the Dog also enjoys good fortune luck in 2008, then the symbolism of the triangle can be further transformed into the sign of the *tai chi* of *yin* and *yang chi*. Note that the Dog's secret friend is the Rabbit and in 2008, the Rabbit enjoys the luck of 8, which is the most auspicious.

Part Three

• FENG SHUI CHART OF 2008

the annual feng shui chart is a map, which reveals the good and bad luck sectors of the home during the year. The chart is created using the *Lo Shu* number of the year. It points to compass locations that are afflicted and in need of cures and remedies. It also reveals the good luck sectors of your home during the coming year.

This practice of time dimension feng shui complements the space and form methods of feng shui practice. It enables practitioners to keep up to date with the changing energies of each new year as the chart reveals afflictions as well as good fortune indications.

The practitioner can move from room to room systematically installing symbolic feng shui cures for rooms/corners affected by bad *chi* energy; and placing suitable enhancers to activate good luck indications.

In the past, old style feng shui consultants would visit homes under their feng shui care to identify afflicted areas. They would use symbolic and ritualistic remedies to immunize residents against the pernicious effects of feng shui afflictions and misfortune stars. Updating feng shui was something left to traditional old masters, as a result of which, it would usually only be the wealthy families who benefited from having updated feng shui. Things are very different these days.

Now with all the necessary information on feng shui updates made easily available each year and with powerful symbolic cures made increasingly available, anyone can update their feng shui themselves.

At World Of Feng Shui, we publicize the annual afflictions and explain how to use the different remedies each year through our popular Feng Shui Extravaganzas. These are live whole day events held in Malaysia and Singapore as well as in the United States and Europe.

The annual and personalized afflictions are also posted on our website *www.wofs.com*. All cures are modern day reproductions of traditional remedies and have become increasingly used by feng shui practitioners who find them very effective for overcoming afflictions.

Each year we research deeper into the almanacs and various feng shui texts from China, Tibet, India and Mongolia to learn more about the metaphysical dimensions of feng shui practice.

THE *LO SHU* NUMBER OF THE YEAR IS 1

In 2008, the year of the Earth Rat, the ruling *Lo Shu* number is the white star 1. So the *Lo Shu* number 1 governs the feng shui chart of the year. This is usually referred to as the triumphant

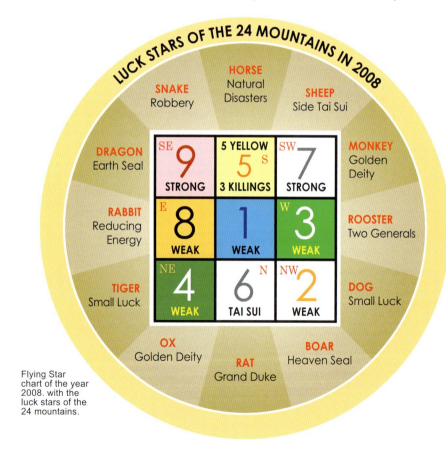

Flying Star chart of the year 2008. with the luck stars of the 24 mountains.

winning star. Unfortunately, star 1 is weak in the center so the year cannot gain fullest advantage from its beneficial aspects. However, the white star 1 signifies water and it represents wealth, so it is generally regarded with great favour.

The number 1 stands for the start of new things and new events, and in the case of 2008, it coincidentally signifies a new calendar cycle as the Rat is the first sign of the Chinese zodiac.

The number 1 can also mean victory in competitive situations. We can say that the year benefits from the favourable number in the center of the chart; however since its energy is weak, not everyone can feel its good effects.

For those born in the year of the Dog, the number 1 has no special significance and the Dog also does not have any special connection to the Rat person.

The problem for 2008 is that when the white star 1 suffers reducing energy, as is the case this year, (its water element is destroyed by the earth element of the center of the chart), the number 1 can thus turn hostile changing from virtuous and positive to non virtuous and negative.

Like a policeman transforming into a gangster and a good man turning into a crook. So element remedies are necessary for 2008. It is only when the white star 1 enjoys strength and vigour that it causes actions directed at us by others, and by us towards others, to be virtuous. When your luck is "virtuous", you will never be a victim and you will rarely be confronted with obstacles.

The number 1 also has a strong effect on the fortunes of the middle son, and when it flies into the center of the chart, it can cause weakness to afflict the middle son. To remedy this, strengthen the North sector of the home with metal energy. Also strengthen your son's intrinsic *chi* by letting him wear something made of gold. Those of you having a hard time dealing with the middle son syndrome can place a metal pagoda in the North.

This year it is beneficial to create metal energy in the center of the home. Metal exhausts Earth and strengthens Water here.

Place Golden Deities such as Fuk Luk Sau in the center of the house. If not in gold, then anything metallic such as brass is also good.

Few Chinese homes would ever do without these auspicious Star Gods, Fuk Luk Sau, whose presence in the home brings health, wealth and prosperity.

THE ILLNESS STAR RESIDES IN THE NORTHWEST

As shown in the chart, 2008's illness star 2 is in the NW. It flies to the place of the Patriarch, but it is weak and does not pose as great a danger as when the star was strong last year. This is because 2 is an Earth star and when it flies into the Northwest, the metal essence of the NW weakens it.

Also, the NW is the place of Heaven energy, which is dominant over Earth energy. This makes the illness star 2 much less of a problem in 2008. Definitely it is less of a threat than it was in the previous year, and certainly the Patriarch of the family will be strong enough to withstand the afflictions of the illness star.

Nevertheless, it is still a good idea to keep it suppressed

through the year by placing all the anti-illness traditional cures in the NW. The feng shui antidote against the illness star is the all metal six-rod windchime which has been used with great success in past years. To be effective, it should have six hollow rods to signify big metal energy.

Windchimes that come with the Wu Lou will do double duty, overcoming illness stars and bringing good health.

Windchimes should not hang directly above your head. If your bedroom is in the NW sector of the house or if your bed is in NW corner of your bedroom, place an all-metal 8 Immortals Wu Lou by the side of your bed. These Taoist saints are associated with magical implements and

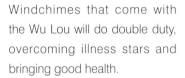

herbs that are believed to have protective and curative powers. An 8 Immortals Wu Lou made of metal in a NW bedroom also activates various types of good fortune for the residents. To some people, they even bring prophetic dreams.

THINGS TO DO IN 2008 IF YOU LIVE IN A NORTHWEST FACING HOUSE

- Keep lights at the front door dim to avoid strengthening the number 2 star.

- Place metal Wu Lou and windchimes in the foyer area to suppress the illness star.

- Protect patriarchal energy with metal element near the main door area.

- Place water at the back of the house to activate the auspicious star 9.

- Paint the door or wall here white to keep the number 2 star suppressed.

- Place a Heaven Seal at the front of a NW3 facing door.

In 2008, the illness star is not strong. Despite this, placing metal in the Northwest to overcome it strengthens the sector, thereby benefiting the man of the house.

In 2008, the subsector NW 1 has small luck so this sub-sector benefit from having its metal energy strengthened. However, the sub-sector NW3 enjoys the Heaven Seal, which brings huge benefits to anyone sleeping or having a desk in this location. So of the three sub-sectors of Northwest, it is the third sub-sector that is the most auspicious based on the luck stars of the 24 mountains.

It is also a good idea to activate the Heaven Seal in this part of the house (or room) by placing the Chinese word *Tien* here indicating heaven. A miniature of the seal placed here is beneficial.

SPECIAL REMEDY FOR 2008'S ILLNESS STAR

You can wear the lapis and gold Medicine Buddha bracelet on your right wrist. This bracelet has the mantra of the Medicine Buddha engraved in pure lapis lazuli on the outside and inside of the bracelet so the mantra is activated by the heat of the human body making it a very powerful amulet and safeguard against illness and premature death.

You can also continue to hang the Medicine Buddha mandala in the house but this time move it to the NW. Doing so brings a double benefit, as the NW is also the place of the Deities. The Medicine Buddha mantra bracelet and mandala invoke powerful healing *chi*, which safeguards the family from illness. It also invokes the blessings of the powerful Medicine Buddha.

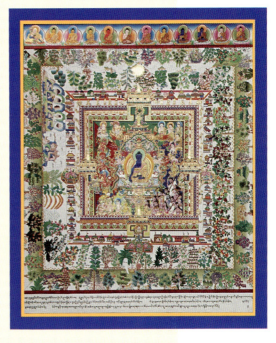

THE HOSTILE STAR RESIDES IN THE WEST

In the coming year, the noisy and quarrelsome star 3 flies to the West, bringing hostile and aggravating energy as well as problems associated with arguments, fights, misunderstandings and court cases, and even serious hostility leading to violence.

Fortunately for anyone having a bedroom in the West sector of the house, the hostile star 3 is weak this year, which is a good thing. This is because being a wood star, the metal element energy of the West presses it down.

In addition to that, the West is visited by the luck star known as Two Generals who not only bring protection to the sector's residents; it also demolishes frivolous arguments and misunderstandings. So in 2008, the luck star of the 24 mountains brings benefit to the West sectors of your house.

The 3 star is a wood element star and the traditional way of overcoming it is to exhaust it with fire element energy. Anything that suggests the fire element can be used. Metal also destroys the quarrelling star, so metal energy is also recommended.

For 2008 we recommend placing images of famous generals - both male and female - in the West, preferably generals dressed in all their gold and scarlet finery. If you like, you can continue to use the traditional remedies against the hostile star 3 such as Laughing Buddhas wearing either gold or

The incredibly auspicious Nine-Dragon screen in 24-carat gold.

red, the gold mandala or colourful Sanskrit yantras. These not only calm the *chi* of the home, they also bring amazing blessings.

To activate the West with good fortune luck, install a Golden nine dragon screen here. This will suppress all the energies that cause others to find fault with you or try to politick against you.

Invoking the nine dragons here means you are using the universal symbol of good fortune, but the Dragon also has significance in 2008, it being the ally of the year's animal sign of the Rat. And because the West is the home of the Rooster (the Dragon's secret friend) this is an acceptable location for the placement of the Dragons.

THINGS TO DO IN 2008 IF YOU LIVE IN A WEST FACING HOUSE

- Do not place water near the front door as this makes the number 3 star stronger.

- Turn on the lights at the front of the house and keep your foyer area well lit.

- Place a Nine Dragon screen on a wall that faces the main door.

- Place water at the back of the house to activate the auspicious star 8.

- Paint the door or wall here red to keep the number 3 star suppressed.

- Place a pair of Generals flanking the door if the door also faces West.

THE SCHOLASTIC STAR RESIDES IN THE NORTHEAST

In 2008 the scholastic and literary star flies to the Northeast. This is signified by the number 4 which is also regarded as a love star associated with peach blossom luck. In this part of the house, the romance aspect of this star benefits the young man.

But in 2008, the peach blossom aspect of the number 4 is weak. This is because the wood 4 is distracted in the NE, a secondary direction not known for strengthening peach blossom. Indeed during 2008, the star number 4 is more effective when activated as a scholastic star.

Here in the NE, the number 4's literary side becomes dominant bringing scholastic and academic luck to those residing in the Northeast. The direction of NE is strongly associated with studies and scholarship.

THINGS TO DO IN 2008 IF YOU LIVE IN A NORTHEAST FACING HOUSE

- Place scholastic symbols like brush and ink near the entrance.

- Place a crystal globe near the entrance to generate scholastic luck.

- Place a Dragon Gate water feature here to jumpstart exam luck.

Thus those occupying this part of the house will benefit from literary and scholastic luck. Fueled as much by the star number as by the NE itself, which favours scholastic pursuits, those still in college or who need study luck will benefit if they activate their NE with all the symbols of scholastic success.

The number 4 is also advantageous for those engaged in the writing and literary professions. Thus Dog -born people who are employed in a writing career or who are in research or the media will benefit from favourable *chi* energy if they are located in the NE part of a house or building.

THE *WU WANG* & THREE KILLINGS RESIDE IN THE SOUTH

In the year 2008, the South sector appears to be rather badly afflicted by a multitude of hardships. This is where the dreaded misfortune star *Wu Wang*, also known as the Five Yellow, resides. This is an earth number, which gets strengthened when it flies into a fire element sector. So the

Five Yellow is to be very much feared this year (unless your Kua number is 5, in which case the Five Yellow might even bring good fortune). For most people and especially for those born in a Horse year, the Five Yellow should be viewed as a pernicious star, which simply must be suppressed.

In addition, the South is also the home of the insidious energy of Three Killings, a suffering burden caused by three types of misfortunes. Anyone hit by this malicious affliction is sure to suffer three types of losses – loss of a loved one, loss of income and loss of good health. It is thus strongly advisable to install powerful remedies that keep the Three Killings under control.

The South is also directly affected by its confrontation with the Grand Duke *Tai Sui*, who in 2008 resides in the opposite direction of North.

These three afflictions cause the South location to be hit by a tornado of feng shui problems to surface. The misfortune brought by them are collectively and individually dangerous, so it is important to pay special attention to the cures required to diffuse all the negative energies hurting the South.

This configuration is lethal for a Rat year, as it suggests danger is coming from the South and thus is directly aimed at the North.

The best cure for anyone with a South-facing main door (or

Kalachakra
mantra plaque

even a secondary door) is to hang the special red Kalachakra mantra plaque above the door. This excellent cure transforms all incoming *shar chi* into benevolent *chi*. It effectively overcomes all malicious energies and is far more powerful than any other cure.

Contained in the Kalachakra symbol and the two mantras on the plaque are wonderful blessings directly extracted from the sutras and anyone walking under these symbols and mantras will receive powerful purifying blessings that instantly dispel all obstacles and hindrances that may be blocking their success.

TO SUPPRESS THE FIVE YELLOW

The feared annual affliction of Five Yellow usually brings a severe illness, accidents and loss in many areas of life. It has the power to trigger different kinds of tragedies and can cause your life to suddenly collapse around you. When you read about disasters striking a family, you can be sure that the Five Yellow is somehow responsible, either because it afflicts the main door or the room the victim occupies. Sometimes, just facing the Five Yellow direction can make one lose energy.

Those of you having main doors, rooms or desks afflicted by the Five Yellow, because they are located in the South, must suppress it before the 4th February 2008. Do not dismiss the Five Yellow and be careless. When bad luck manifests, it might be too late to do something about it. Prevention is better than cure; do not wait until it is too late to repair a bad situation.

The bad news for 2008 is that because the South is a fire

element location, the Five Yellow is very strong. When the Five Yellow is strong, it creates violent misfortune such as severe business loss or severe terminal illness. In 2008, the Five Yellow operates at a magnified level. You should treat the South location of your home with great care.

Definitely the antidote against the Five Yellow - the five element pagoda - must be immediately placed in the South. Those whose houses face North also need the five element pagoda, as these houses are said to be sitting South. In such houses, the pagoda should be placed at

The five element pagoda is the perfect cure for the Five Yellow.

NOTE

The five element pagoda is an incredibly powerful remedy for the Five Yellow during the period of 8. It is the cure recommended in many of the texts on flying star feng shui as being particularly strong during an Earth period. Period 8 is an Earth period.

To make your pagoda do its job more efficiently, place some garden soil (taken from your own house) inside the pagoda. This signifies imprisoning the earth energy of the Five Yellow wherever the pagoda is placed. If you live in an apartment, get the earth from a potted plant inside your home or borrow some earth from the garden of your condo building.

the back of the house. This ensures the home is adequately insulated against the Five Yellow.

If you reside in a room that is located in the South, you should protect yourself by installing any of the remedies that exhaust the Five Yellow. Do this at the start of the year. Hang a six-rod all-metal windchime in the South corner of your room. Most important is to display the all-metal five-element pagoda in the same corner. These cures are excellent for suppressing the dangerous *chi* of the Five Yellow.

Those who have used this cure last year can recycle their pagodas, although new ones are preferable as the energy of new windchimes and new pagodas is always so much stronger. If you are recycling, do re-energize your cures by washing them with natural

salt and keeping them in the sun for seven straight days. Then let them stand in the outdoors for three more days, absorbing the natural yang energy of the environment.

Dog people belong to the earth element, so Dog people are better able to withstand the Five Yellow of the South. Nevertheless in 2008, you should make certain you are not in any way afflicted by this powerful misfortune star.

Those of you exposed in any way to the South sector of your home should still place the cures suggested. It does not harm to temporarily move out of the South room to another room should you so wish and are able to do so.

TO SUPPRESS THE THREE KILLINGS

In 2008, the South is also host to the nasty Three Killings affliction. Through 2008, this affliction can bring all kinds of situations to annoy and upset anyone occupying a room located here. If you occupy the South sector of your house, you will be a suffering victim of gossip, slander and politicking, all of a serious nature that can lead to aggravations and problems. You can also experience loss and misfortune.

The celestial protectors - the Fu Dog, Chi Lin and Pi Yao - overcome the Three Killings affliction.

Unless you place cures to effectively suppress the Three Killings, you are sure to suffer the nasty consequences arising from this affliction. The Three Killings often derail the best laid plans as they cause unexpected obstacles that slow you down. Everyone must keep the Three Killings under control. It must also be remembered not to undertake renovations where the Three Killings occur, so in 2008, no digging, cutting or drilling in the South!

The best way to keep the Three Killings under control is the presence of the three celestial protectors – comprising the Chi Lin, the Fu Dog and the Pi Yao. Lined up together, these three protective creatures create a sufficiently powerful invisible wall of protective energy that ensures the Three Killings cannot penetrate the energy of the home through the South.

If there is a window in your South, keep it closed or at least have the curtains drawn shut, especially in the afternoons when sunlight is strong and penetrating.

DO NOT RENOVATE THE SOUTH IN 2008

It is imperative that everyone observes the NO RENOVATION rule for the South during 2008. Undertaking any kind of demolition work is dangerous as this activates the negative luck to manifest in this sector. It is especially dangerous to drill floors, knock down walls, dig holes in the ground, engage in any kind of destructive work or make too much noise. When any of these activities are carried out, you are activating the Five Yellow of the sector and this is what triggers severe misfortune luck to manifest. So the best thing you can do is keep the South as quiet as possible.

Those building something in the South will not be activating the *chi* here, but it is never advisable to create anything at a time when the space is afflicted. Hence better to postpone whatever building you may be planning for the South sector to the following year.

THINGS TO DO IN 2008 IF YOU LIVE IN A SOUTH FACING HOUSE

- Place five element pagoda at the front of the house to exhaust the Five Yellow.

- Keep front lights of the house turned off if possible.

- Place water at the back of the house to activate the heaven luck of 6.

- Place the three celestial protectors at the front – Chi Lin, Fu Dog and Pi Yao.

- Keep the front door quiet, dimly lit and use another door if possible.

THE WHITE STAR SIX & *TAI SUI* RESIDE IN THE NORTH

In the coming year, the luck of the North is excellent as it enjoys the divine luck of 6. This sector enjoys the kind of luck generally associated with unexpected windfalls such as an inheritance, winning the lottery or collecting, and receiving cash you had long given up on.

The white star number 6 is associated with the powerful Trigram *Chien*, which stands for the Patriarch. It also stands for heaven. To many masters of feng shui, the number 6 signifies gold, which is the king of metal, so when the number 6 enters into any location, its "face" or appearance always suggests riches and prosperity. The number 6 is therefore highly prized.

In the Constellation of the Dipper, the number 6 represents finance and everything to do with money. At its most positive, 6 represents high authority, influence and great riches – almost like a finance minister. When the number 6 appears in the North however, it tends to show its weak nature, although in Period 8, this is not something we need to worry about too much.

This star 6 is also known as the military star, which means it has the potential to bring promotion and mentor luck. So you will have a guardian angel watching over the North sector in 2008. The projects you are planning and working on will bring great success and proceed smoothly and with few obstacles.

Luck brought by the number 6 is usually not big time money luck, but it brings happy feelings. Those living in the North can activate this sector with water. This actualizes success and prosperity and ensures plenty of upward mobility for the residents of the family.

Other suitable decorative items that benefit from being placed in the North are golden images of tortoises, Pi Yaos and other celestial creatures.

Any kind of tortoises will bring longevity and harmonious luck for the family. These can be painted in all colours and made of different materials.

Place six tortoises here to activate the lucky number. It is also very auspicious to place Pi Yaos in the North in 2008 as this takes advantage of the presence of the God of the

Year here. This is the *Tai Sui* or Grand Duke Jupiter.

In 2008, the *Tai Sui* is housed in the second subsector of the North direction. Here, the *Tai Sui* is occupying the sector of the Rat, which adds another dimension to the feng shui of the North.

The tortoise brings longevity and harmony for the family.

THE *TAI SUI* OF 2008

The *Tai Sui* of 2008 is the Grand Duke *Zhou Dang* of the Ming Dynasty. His origins are humble but he rose to become an important Minister in the Government of the Emperor.

This Grand Duke is known to favour those with good character and who are honest, compassionate and efficient. He has good control over troublemakers and generally brings peace and harmony to the year. This *Tai Sui* does not bring wealth but rather is known more for his noble character and for his ability to bring compromise, harmony and peace.

Confronting the Grand Duke always brings misfortune, failure and loss. Even if the North is an excellent direction for you, it is better in 2008 to face another direction, especially when it comes to sitting at the office desk. When you confront the *Tai Sui*, nothing you do can succeed smoothly, there will always be obstacles cropping up unexpectedly.

Be careful of this feng shui taboo in 2008 as you don't want your good fortune to get blocked by the Grand Duke. So do not face the North direction all through 2008.

Here is where placing beautiful Pi Yaos in the North is so beneficial. These celestial chimeras are very effective in soothing the nerves of the Grand Duke Jupiter. Get them in black or any dark colour to enhance their power against a background of heavenly energies.

**In 2008 it is better not to sit facing
the South/North axis, as doing so will bring
plenty of difficulties and misfortune.
In 2008 everyone must avoid sitting
or facing North or South.**

One of the taboos of feng shui is never to disturb the Grand Duke. This means that his place of residence during the year must be undisturbed. You must not renovate where he resides so no renovations, drilling, banging and knocking down walls or digging holes in the ground is allowed in the North in 2008.

Generally the rule is not to engage in any demolition work at all. For those thinking of starting renovations in 2008 to change to a Period 8 house, the advice is to give the North sector a miss. If you need to renovate this part of your house, either delay till the following year or start (and end) renovations in another more auspicious sector.

THE BURGLARY AFFLICTION RESIDES IN THE SOUTHWEST

In 2008, the "place of potential violence and burglary" hurts the Matriarchal direction. This affliction of the Southwest direction is caused by the presence of the number 7 here.

The number 7 attracts violence, political turmoil and generally brings out the worst in all of us. Its presence in any sector is sure to spark aggressive behavior that could potentially ignite into something dangerous.

Coming to the SW, the 7 star is made stronger, thereby making it really lethal and potent. This is because the earth element energy of the SW fuels the element energy of the 7 star. The best way to overcome its negative effects is to have a large water feature here, as water is what exhausts the vigour of the 7 star.

Those of you who already have a water feature in the SW (a pool or a pond here) to activate the indirect spirit of the current Period of 8 will be happy to know that in addition to generating wealth luck, the pool or pond is also suppressing the burglary star. This is an added bonus here for you in 2008 as the pool creates an invisible protective shield.

The blue rhino to combat the number 7 burglary star.

For those who have a door here and do not have a pond here, they might want to try using an urn of water.

Place this water cure in the SW corner of your living room or in the garden in 2008. Also place a rhinoceros image here to strengthen the cure.

A rhino with two horns is stronger than a single horned rhino. This will help to safeguard you from getting cheated or robbed. If your do not have a door in the SW, this affliction should not hurt you unless you are sleeping in a SW-located room. Then the advice is to carry a blue rhino with you at all times.

THINGS TO DO IN 2008 IF YOU LIVE IN A SOUTHWEST FACING HOUSE

- Display a pair of double horned rhinoceros flanking your front door on the outside.

- Place a water feature at the front of the house either just inside or outside the door.

- Paint your front wall blue to simulate water *chi*.

- Place a golden deity at the front door if it is facing SW3.

- Place a pair of Pi Yao at the front of the door if it is facing SW1 to overcome the side affliction with the *Tai Sui*.

THE AUSPICIOUS *CHI* OF 8 RESIDES IN THE EAST

In 2008, the most auspicious sector of the home is the East, which enjoys the presence of the auspicious number 8 star. Its earth element however makes it weak this year because in flying into a wood sector, it gets weakened. Wood destroys Earth.

The weakened 8 means that it is not as robust in bringing wealth luck and it must be strengthened with the presence of bright lights. This is very important because the East 2 direction is also visited by the luck star of reducing energy. This seriously lowers the power of 8 in 2008.

Nevertheless, the number 8 is always regarded as a very lucky number, and it continues to be very lucky all through the current period, which ends only on February 4th 2024.

In fact, the number 8, which is also a white star, is currently in its brightest period. As a lucky star, it beats all other numbers. This comes once in 180 years, so it is advisable to take fullest advantage of the number 8 in the current Period of 8.

To activate the luck of number 8 however, it should be soaked in yang energy wherever it appears and this means lots of activity, lots of noise and plenty of bright lights. When there is movement, sound and activity, the number 8 brings a great deal of good fortune. In the Constellation, 8 is a "man-made star" with two assistants – a right and a left assistant.

At its most positive, the number 8 signifies great wealth, honesty as well as great nobility and in the current period of 8, the youngest son of any family will rise to great prominence. In a family of three or five sons, watch the youngest son, for he will have great success in Period 8.

At its most negative however or when it gets afflicted either by harmful structures in the environment (such as big buildings made of wood or are painted red in colour) or by the presence of excessive metal energy, the number 8 can bring harm to young children especially young sons, causing severe sickness to manifest. However, this is unlikely to happen in the current period, as its *chi* energy is very strong. The number 8 will only manifest its negative side after 4th February 2024.

In the current period the number 8 is magnificently auspicious in any guise or combination. Even when just worn as personal adornment, the number, or rather its symbol, attracts wealth and this is because in

THINGS TO DO IN 2008 IF YOU LIVE IN AN EAST FACING HOUSE

- Install bright lights in the East to strengthen the number 8 star

- Simultaneously also have bright lights at the back of the house

- Place Green Dragons here to strengthen the luck of the eldest son

- Use the door located in the East as frequently as possible

- Use the front door here as often as possible to generate yang *chi*

shape it resembles the infinity sign. Repeated three times, the 8 becomes the incredibly auspicious mystical knot.

In 2008, the number 8 entering the East favours the eldest son. Since this is the period of the young man, sons of families benefit tremendously if they occupy rooms located in the East sector. The year favours the young man in the same way the Period of 8 does, so this is a year when all young men should go bravely forth and do their thing!

The East is the home direction of the Rabbit, so the auspicious number 8 found here benefits the Rabbit born and its allies, the Sheep and the Boar as well as its secret friend the Dog. The East is also the place of the Green Dragon, so placing images of dragons here will activate the 8 and cause it to attract excellent feng shui into the home.

THE PURPLE STAR OF COMPLETION RESIDES IN THE SOUTHEAST

In 2008, the luck of future prosperity signified by the number 9 flies to the Southeast. Here we see the fire element flying into a sector of wood element, so in this sector it can be interpreted to mean that the wood strengthens the fire, so 9 is strong here.

Generally, the presence of the number 9 star brings the luck of future prosperity as well as the luck of completion, so it benefits those working on specific projects.

The energy of this location helps you overcome obstacles that may be standing in your way. If you have outstanding matters left over from the previous year, this is a favourable sector for you to work in to finish your project in a satisfactory way. The luck of completion is a very significant kind of luck, as it brings a good ending to anything you start. This star number also benefits those starting new ventures as the energy of 9 favours building for future prosperity.

Those whose front doors face Southeast will benefit from the 9 and also from the luck stars that fly into this sector. The SE1 direction benefits from the Earth Seal, which brings luck in real estate ventures. It will help all those benefiting from this direction to accumulate assets. If you activate this area by shining bright lights here, the benefits of the Earth Seal will manifest more speedily.

The SE3 direction also benefits as the luck star brings the Golden door guardians. According to legend, this brings protection against unexpected bad luck, ensuring a smooth year for those enjoying the benefit of this direction.

THINGS TO DO IN 2008 IF YOU LIVE IN A SOUTHEAST FACING HOUSE

- Place water at the front of the house to activate *sheng chi* luck.

- Keep the front of the house brightly lit to activate completion luck of 9.

- Hang windchimes at the back of the house to suppress the illness star 2.

- Activate Earth Seal in front and Heaven Seal at the back of the house.

- Display nine glitter lamps in the living room facing the front door.

- Display nine dragons facing the front door.

Part Three

- **PRODUCTS TO ENHANCE LUCK IN 2008**

ACTIVATE ALLIES & SECRET FRIENDS LUCK

The Dog belongs to the INDEPENDENTS group of affinity made up of the Dog, the Tiger and the Horse. These three animal signs are allies. They have key attitudes in common such as being rebellious free spirits who are as proud as they are determined. They can be showy and rather boastful, but they are people with substance.

Amongst the zodiac animals they are the most charismatic. The Horse leads while the Tiger strategizes and the Dog makes friends. Together they can be formidable. The problem in 2008 is that the Horse is seriously afflicted this year. As such there is a weak link in this particular triangle.

This grouping is hard pressed to create the triangle of trinity within their homes yet it is important to do so. Of the three, it is the Tiger who is the strongest in 2008, but he is distracted, so this is a grouping

The Dog's allies are the Tiger and the Horse, while the secret friend is the Rabbit. Have images of these animal signs near you in 2008.

that is not at its best in 2008. To strengthen this affinity triangle it is necessary to borrow the luck of the Rabbit who is the secret friend of the Dog. So placing images of the Rabbit and lighting up the East direction in your home is an excellent thing to do. During the year, the Dog is better off not wearing anything but its own image. To strengthen the South however, it is beneficial to place lots of horses there as this brings the strength of numbers. But do keep the South dimly lit.

AUSPICIOUS GOLD JEWELLERY FOR 2008

In 2008, the Dog person would benefit from increasing the amount of metal element as the year suffers a shortage of metal. In terms of auspicious gold jewellery, here are three things most beneficial to the Dog person:

- The Yin and Yang mantra bracelet, which brings powerful cures that keep the illness affliction, subdued but more importantly has the power to enhance the 24 mountains star of small luck. This bracelet also helps maintain the Dog person's balance in a year which tends to bring imbalance and aggravations caused by a weakened affinity triangle. This bracelet will also tap into the secret forces of the mantras of the bracelet and reciting the wish-fulfilling mantra will bring plenty of benefits.

The Omani Padme Hum pendant

- For those wanting to find love and a soul mate it is a good idea to wear one of the five element mantra rings. The Dog person tends to be impulsive in love this year and wearing mantra ring will have a steadying effect on your emotions. For those wanting success, select the Green Tara mantra ring as this will help you actualise all your wishes swiftly.

- The Dog should also wear a mantra pendant and we suggest the Omani Padme Hum pendant. This brings spiritual and temporal protection for the Dog person, especially from too easily opening his/her heart to new people in his/her life. The Omani pendant affords some measure of protection and blessings.

AUSPICIOUS GOLD DEITIES TO DISPLAY

In 2008, the luck star influencing the fortunes of Dog is the Small Luck star, so what is needed are the deities that can boost Dog's small luck into big luck. For prosperity, the Dog benefits from displaying one of the following:

- the golden God of Wealth is very auspicious for the NW1 location.

- the golden Fuk Luk Sau in the dining room.
- the Ksiddhigarbha placed behind you at work to help enhance business luck.

The Chinese believe that inviting Taoist or Buddhist deities into the home is a very auspicious thing to do, although this is also a very personal matter as it might not be suitable for those whose religion has other deities. This is entirely up to them – For instance, those who wish to do so can look for deities from their own pantheon of Gods. We recommend Taoist and Buddhist deities simply because we are familiar with them, but it is perfectly acceptable to invite in other deities that you are familiar with. But it is advisable to gold leaf them as the metal element of gold is most auspicious in 2008.

Kuan Kung

BEST SEMI-PRECIOUS STONES & COLOURS FOR 2008

In 2008, the Dog benefits from wearing citrines and other yellow coloured stones such as yellow sapphires and diamonds. There aren't many yellow gemstones available and there are even fewer that are affordable. Citrine is a wonderful option that offers a wide range of colour in the yellow spectrum. When buying gem quality citrines you can assume you are getting a heat-treated stone but this is perfectly acceptable. Another great gemstone for the Dog to wear in 2008 is the deep yellow Topaz.

Those Dogs wanting to generate speculative luck or to be able to collect debts long owed to them should wear the powerful and colourless diamond. Make sure to get one that has a lot of inner fire. The better it sparkles,

the more effective it will be, especially for those needing to collect debts owed to them. Dog women benefit from wearing yellow diamonds as these signify their intrinsic element of earth. In 2008, wearing these earth coloured gemstone can be extremely beneficial.

To overcome the illness star, Dog people should also wear lapis lazuli beads or a lapis pendant. In the past this gemstone was very popular as a stone that could ward off illness and other terminal type of diseases. The Medicine Buddha is said to be the King of lapis light and the blue light is a powerful healing light. You can also get the Medicine Buddha bracelet where the mantra is created with pure crushed blue lapis.

GO FOR 3,6 OR 9-EYED DZI BEAD IN 2008

In 2008, the Dog should check out Dzi beads that have three, six or nine eyes. The 3-eyed Dzi will bring luck in business opportunities while the 6-eyed Dzi attracts speculative luck. Those who indulge in speculative ventures will benefit from wearing the 6-eyed Dzi bead.

To maximize your wealth luck and potential in 2008, it is beneficial to wear the 9-eyed Dzi bead. This brings many unexpected opportunities into the Dog person's life opening new doorways.

When choosing Dzi beads, look for beads that are fat and cylindrical. They should also feel smooth to the touch. Never wear oversized Dzi beads as these are fake and often made of cheap paste material.

The best place to wear Dzi beads are either around the neck as pendants, in which case they should touch the

3-eyed Dzi

9-eyed Dzi

throat or heart chakra (i.e. they should touch the flesh) or on the wrist as bracelets. Wear them with crystals or citrines on your right wrist (if you wish to receive money) with the bead touching your pulse point.

You will find that the Dzi bead will make things go smoothly for you all year round. Those in business will experience their deals moving along with no hitch and they will also attract a new set of customers.

If you are the kind who wants to have more than one bead, you can string three Dzi beads into a necklace and wear under your shirt, allowing the beads to touch your heart chakra. This expands your mental creativity and helps you make good choices. Tibetans wear Dzi beads as amulets and talismans, although wearing a Dzi is also a kind of status symbol. Dzi beads there are usually passed on from father to son or from mothers to daughters and rarely do families part with their Dzi beads. Remember that the more you wear your Dzi beads, the better they will bond with your personal energy.

DRAGON CARP FOUNTAIN

For the young Dog student, this is an excellent year to create the fabulous luck of the Dragon Gate or *lung men* – especially if you have an important exam or are applying for a scholarship. Those just finishing their tertiary education and looking to start a career should also activate the luck of the Dragon Gate.

The Dragon Gate is reputed to be high up in the mountains, at the source of a great river where carps become dragons upon successfully jumping across the Dragon Gate. This signifies successfully passing your examinations and finding yourself a good job, one that sets you on course for a great career.

Having water in your Dragon Carp Fountain will be thus be most auspicious in ensuring this. This is one of the best feng shui enhancers for generating education luck. Place in the Dog direction of NW1 to maximize the benefits of this enhancer.

A Dragon Gate water feature brings examination luck and success to the second generation when placed in the Northeast of the living room.

Get all your feng shui good fortune symbols from
WORLD OF FENG SHUI boutiques worldwide:

MALAYSIA

WOFS MID VALLEY
Lot T-016, Centre Court, 3rd Floor,
Mid Valley Megamall, Mid Valley City,
Lingkaran Syed Putra,
59200 KL, Malaysia.
Tel: +603-2287 9975 Fax: +603-2287 9975
Email: wofs@worldoffengshui.com

WOFS NORTHPOINT
A-17-1, 17th Floor, Northpoint Office,
Northpoint Mid Valley City, No:1,
Medan Syed Putra Utara, 59200, Kuala Lumpur.
Tel: +603-2080 3488 Fax: +603-2287 4813
Email: wofs@worldoffengshui.com

WOFS CENTRAL MARKET
M34, Mezzanine Floor, Central Market,
Jalan Hang Kasturi, 50050 KL.
Tel: +603-2274 8096
Email: wofs@worldoffengshui.com

WOFS KEPONG
Lot G09, Ground Floor, Jusco Metro Prima Shopping Centre,
No.1, Jalan Metro Prima,
52100 Kepong, KL Boutique. Tel: +603-6250 0728
Email: wofs@worldoffengshui.com

WOFS BUKIT RAJA
Lot F17, Jusco Bukit Raja, Persiaran Bukit Raja 2,
Bandar Baru Klang, 41150 Klang.
Tel: +603-3341 3889
Fax: +603-3341 7889
Email: bukitraja@worldoffengshui.com

WOFS GURNEY
170-04-50, Plaza Gurney, Persiaran Gurney,
10250 Penang, Malaysia.
Tel: +604-228 4618 Fax: +604-228 7618
Email: gurney@worldoffengshui.com

WOFS IPOH
76, Jalan Theatre, 30300 Ipoh, Perak
Tel: +605-249 2688   Fax:+605-242 0688
E-mail: ipoh@worldoffengshui.com

WOFS KOTA KINABALU
Lot B205, 2nd Floor, Phase II,
Wisma Merdeka,
Jln Tun Razak, 88000 Kota Kinabalu, Sabah.
Tel: +088-248 798 Fax: +088-247 798
Email: kotakinabalu@worldoffengshui.com

WOFS KUANTAN
Berjaya Megamall, Lot 23(i), Ground floor,
MainConcourse, JalanTun Ismail,
Sri Dagangan,25000 Kuantan,
Pahang Darul Makmur
Email: kuantan@worldoffengshui.com

WOFS KUCHING
No. 289, Ground Floor, Sub-Lot 1,
Wisma Ho Ho Lim, Jalan Abell,
93100, Kuching, Sarawak, East Malaysia.
Tel: +082-425 698 Fax: +082-424 698
Email: kuching@worldoffengshui.com

WOFS MELAKA
Lot F51/F52, Mahkota Parade,
No 1 Jalan Merdeka, 75000 Melaka.
Tel: +606-282 2688 Fax: +606-283 1288
Email: melaka@worldoffengshui.com

WOFS MIRI
Lot 1.26, Level 1, Bintang Plaza,
Miri/Pujut Road, 98000 Miri, Sarawak.
Tel: +6085-439168 Fax: +6085-417198
Email: miri@worldoffengshui.com

WOFS PUCHONG
Lot S10, 2nd Floor, IOI Mall,
Batu 9 Jalan Puchong,
Bandar Puchong Jaya,
47100 Puchong, Selangor.
Tel: +603-5882 2652 Fax: +603-5882 2653
Email: puchong@worldoffengshui.com

WOFS QUEENSBAY
2F-120 (Central Zone), Queensbay Mall,
11900 Bayan Lepas, Penang.
Tel: +604-659 5688 Fax: +604-659 5688
E-mail: queensbay@worldoffengshui.com

WOFS SEREMBAN
Lot F32, 1st Floor,
Jusco Shopping Centre Seremban 2,
No 112, Persiaran S2, B1 Seremban 2,
70300 Seremban.
Tel: +606-601 3088 Fax: +606-601 3092
E-mail: seremban@worldoffengshui.com

WOFS SUBANG
Lot G24B, Ground Floor,
Subang Parade, 5,
Jalan SS16/1, Subang Jaya,
47500 Petaling Jaya, Selangor, Malaysia.
Tel: +603-5632 1428
Fax: +603-5632 0378
Email: subang@worldoffengshui.com

WOFS TAIPING
12A, Jalan Taiping 2, Off Jalan Tupai,
Taiping Business Centre,
34000 Taiping, Perak.
Tel: +605-806 6648 Fax: +605-807 6648
E-mail: taiping@worldoffengshui.com

WOFS TEBRAU
Lot S12, 2nd Floor,
Aeon Tebrau Shopping City Shopping Centre
No 1, Jalan Desa Tebrau, Taman Desa Tebrau,
81100 Johor Bahru, Johor.
Tel: +607-357 9968
E-mail: johor@worldoffengshui.com

WOFS MUTIARA
Mutiara Hotel Johor Bahru
Lot 07, Shopping Arcade, Ground Floor, Jalan Dato
Sulaiman, Taman Century,
80990 Johor Bahru
Tel: +607-331 9968   Fax: +607-387 8968
Email; johor@worldoffengshui.com

AUSTRALIA
WOFS MELBOURNE
Lower Ground Floor, Crown Entertainment Complex,
(One level below the food court) 8 Whiteman St,
Southbank 3006, Melbourne, Victoria, Australia.
Tel: +613-9645-8588 Fax: +613-9645-8588
Email: melbourne@worldoffengshui.com

BELGIUM
WOFS BELGIUM
Ninoofsesteenweg 1072, BE-1080 Brussels, Belgium.
Tel: +32 02 522 2697
Fax: +32 02 569 0123
Email: belgium@worldoffengshui.com

BRUNEI
WOFS BRUNEI
No. 7, Blk B, 1st Floor, Warisan Mata-mata Gadong BSB,
BE1718 Brunei Darussalam.
Tel: +673-245 4977
Fax: +673-242 1876
Email: brunei@worldoffengshui.com

CANADA
WOFS TORONTO
3175, Rutherford Road, Unit 24, Tuscany Place at Vaughan
Mills, Vaughan, Ontario L4K 5Y6, Canada.
Tel: +1 905 660 8899   Fax: +1 905 660 8809
E-mail: toronto@worldoffengshui.com

GUATEMALA
WOFS GUATEMALA
Galerias La Pradera, 25-85, Zona 10,
2 do nivel local 252 "B" Guatemala, Guatemala
E-mail: guatemala@worldoffengshui.com

INDIA
WOFS CALCUTTA
74, Shakespeare Sarani, Calcutta, 700017, India.
Email: calcutta@worldoffengshui.com

INDONESIA
WOFS ARTHA GADING
Artha Gading Mall, Gramedia Book Store Level 2,
Block B3/1A, Jln. Boulevard, Artha Gading Selatan
No. 1 Kelapa Gading, Jakarta-Utara 14240.
Tel: +6221-668 3610/20/30
Fax: +6221-668 9625
Email: indonesia@worldoffengshui.com

WOFS KELAPA GADING
Kelapa Gading Plaza Blok M Lt. II JL. Kelapa Gading
Boulevard, Jakarta Utara 14240 Indonesia.
Tel: +6221-4526986
Fax: +6221-4526977
Email: indonesia@worldoffengshui.com

WOFS MATRAMAN
Toko Buku Gramedia Matraman, Matraman Jaya,
no: 46-50, Jakarta Timur, Indonesia.
Tel: +6221-8517325 Fax: +6221-8517325
Email: indonesia@worldoffengshui.com

WOFS MTA
Mall Taman Anggrek (MTA) Ground Level Lt. G16-19,
Jalan Letjen S. Parman Kav. 21, Slipi-Jakarta Barat,
Indonesia. Tel: +6221-5699-9488
Fax: +6221-5699-9577
Email: indonesia@worldoffengshui.com

JAPAN
WOFS JAPAN
Takigen Building 5th Floor 1-24-4, Nishi-Gotanda Shinagawa-ku
Tokyo, Zip141-0031 Japan
Tel: +81-3-5926-4698
Fax: +81-3-5926-4697
Email: japan@worldoffengshui.com

WOFS MIE
670-2 Shinmei Ago-Cho Shima-City, Mie, 517-0502, Japan.
Tel: +81-599-43-8909
Fax: +81-599-46-0178
Email: mie@worldoffengshui.com

NETHERLANDS
WOFS NETHERLANDS
Stationsplein 1, 1404 Am Bussum, Netherlands.
Tel: +31-356781838 Fax: +31-356783668
Email: netherlands@worldoffengshui.com

PHILIPPINES
WOFS CEBU
Unit 023B, Lower Ground Floor, SM City Cebu,
Cebu Citu, Philippines. Tel/Fax: +63-2231 4088
E-mail: philippines@worldoffengshui.com

WOFS PODIUM
Ground Floor, The Podium, 18 ADB Avenue, Ortigas Center,
Mandaluyong City, Metro Manila, 1605 Philippines.
Tel: +63-29106000
Fax: +63-29106001
Email: philippines@worldoffengshui.com

WOFS MOA
Mall of Asia (MOA) SM Mall of Asia,
SM Central Business Park I, Island A, Bay City, Pasag City
Tel: +63-2910 6000
Fax: + 63-2910 6001
Email: philippines@worldoffengshui.com

WOFS SM NORTH EDSA
The Block, Quezon City, Philippines.
Tel: +63-9106337   Email: philippines@worldoffengshui.com

WOFS SERENDRA
The Piazza, Fort Bonifacio, Global City, Philippines.
Tel: +63-856 0669 Email: philippines@worldoffengshui.com

RUSSIA
WOFS MOSCOW
Office 6-8, Building 519, Russian Exhibition Center, Moscow,
129515, Russian Federation.
Email: moscow@worldoffengshui.com

SPAIN
WOFS BARCELONA
C.Urgell, 40, 08011, Barcelona, Spain.
Tel: +34934244801 Fax: +34934239313
Email: spain@worldoffengshui.com

WOFS MADRID
Centro Comercial Mercado Puerta de Toledo,
Local 3341, Ronda de Toledo, No.1, Madrid, Spain.
Tel: +34-91-3642771 Fax: +34-91-7346400
Email: madrid@worldoffengshui.com

WOFS VALENCIA
Calle Joaquin Costa 53, 46005, Valencia, Spain.
E-mail: valencia@worldoffengshui.com